# A Cheesemonger's Compendium of British and Irish Cheeses

First published in Great Britain in 2021 by

Profile Books
29 Cloth Fair
London EC1A 7JQ

www.profilebooks.com


1 3 5 7 9 10 8 6 4 2

Typeset in Berkeley Old Style and Gill Sans
to a design by Henry Iles.

A CIP catalogue record for this book is available from the
British Library.

ISBN 978-1788167154
eISBN 978-1782838098


Printed in China by 1010 Printing
on FSC®(Forest Stewardship Council®) certified paper

# A Cheesemonger's Compendium of British and Irish Cheeses

## Ned Palmer

Illustrations
**Claire Littlejohn**

Gazetteer
**Dominic Beddow**

# Contents

Introduction                                                   7

## Fresh cheeses                                              13

Ballyhubbock Sheep's Halloumi 18; Clerkland Crowdie 19; Cote
Hill White 20; Kedar Mozzarella 21; Pant Ys Gawn 22; Perroche 23;
Yorkshire Fettle 24.

## Mould-ripened cheeses                                     25

Ailsa Craig 33; Angiddy 34; Baron Bigod 35; Bix 36; Brefu Bach
37; Cavanbert 38; Cenarth Brie 39; Corleggy Kid 40; Dorstone 41;
Elmhirst 42; Elrick Log 43; Flower Marie 44; Golden Cross 45;
Hebden 46; Little She 47; Lord London 48; Ragstone 49; Saint George
50; Saint Jude 51; Saint Tola 52; Saint Tola Ash 53; Sinodun Hill 54;
The Cheese With No Name 55; Tor 56; Triple Rose 57; Tunworth 58;
Wicklow Bán 59; Wigmore 60; Winslade 61; Witheridge 62.

## Blue cheeses                                              63

Barkham Blue 70; Bath Blue 71; Beauvale Blue 72; Beenleigh Blue
73; Binham Blue 74; Blue Monk 75; Bluemin White 76; Boyne Valley
Blue 77; Buffalo Blue 78; Burt's Blue 79; Cashel Blue 80; Colston
Bassett Stilton 81; Cote Hill Blue 82; Crozier Blue 83; Darling Blue
84; Dorset Blue Vinney 85; Hebridean Blue 86; Lanark Blue 87;
Leeds Blue 88; Ludlow Blue 89; Mon Las Anglesey Blue 90; Mrs
Bell's Blue 91; Oxford Blue 92; Remembered Hills 93; Shropshire
Blue 94; Sparkenhoe Blue 95; Stichelton 96; Wicklow Blue 97;
Young Buck 98.

## Washed-rind cheeses 99

Admiral Collingwood 105; Baronet 106; Drewi Sant 107; Durrus 108; Edmund Tew 109; Eve 110; Gubbeen 111; Highmoor 112; Lindum 113; Little Rollright 114; Maida Vale 115; Merry Wyfe of Bath 116; Milleens 117; Ogleshield 118; Oxford Isis 119; Rachel 120; Renegade Monk 121; Saint Cera 122; Saint James 123; Saval 124; Stinking Bishop 125; Westray Wife 126.

## Semi-soft cheeses 127

Caerfai Caerffili 132; Carlow Farmhouse 133; Cornish Yarg 134; Crookwheel 135; Crump's Single Gloucester 136; Cuddy's Cave 137; Duckett's Caerphilly 138; Dunmanus 139; Fellstone (Whin Yeats Wensleydale) 140; Gorwydd Caerphilly 141; Martell's Single Gloucester 142; Monkland 143; Moorland Tomme 144; Old Roan 145; Rainton Tomme 146; Richard III Wensleydale 147; Rockfield 148; Seator's Orkney 149; Stonebeck Wensleydale 150; Stoney Cross 151; Suffolk Gold 152; Thelma's Caerffili 153; Ticklemore 154; Wiltshire Loaf 155; Yorkshire Pecorino 156.

## Hard cheeses 157

Allerdale 164; Anster 165; Appleby's Cheshire 166; Berkswell 167; Bermondsey Hard Pressed 168; Cais Na Tire 169; Cerwyn Mature 170; Clonmore 171; Coolattin 172; Coolea 173; Corra Linn 174; Crump's Double Gloucester 175; Cumberland Farmhouse 176; Derg Cheddar 177; Doddington 178; Drumlin 179; Dunlop 180; Fifteen Fields 181; Goatisan 182; Hafod 183; Hardy's 184; Hegarty's Cheddar 185; Isle of Mull Cheddar 186; Keen's Cheddar 187; Killeen 188; Kirkham's Lancashire 189; Kit Calvert Wensleydale 190; Lincolnshire Poacher 191; Little Hereford 192; Loch Arthur 193; Lord of the Hundreds 194; Martell's Double Gloucester 195; Mayfield 196; Montgomery's Cheddar 197; Mossfield 198; Norfolk Dapple 199; Old Winchester 200; Owd Ewe 201; Pitchfork Cheddar 202; Quicke's Cheddar 203; St Andrews 204; Saint Gall 205; Shropshire 206; Sparkenhoe Red Leicester 207; Spenwood 208; Summerfield 209; Teifi 210; Templegall 211; Tinto 212; Wells Alpine 213; Westcombe Cheddar 214.

Choosing cheese 217; Tasting cheese 218; How much to buy 220; How long to keep cheese 220; A great cheeseboard 221; Serving cheese 223; What to drink with cheese 224; A little Welsh rarebit 225.

**Index of cheesemakers** . . . . . . . . . . . . . . . . . . . . . . . . . . . . . . .228

**Index of cheeses** . . . . . . . . . . . . . . . . . . . . . . . . . . . . . . . . . . .231

**Cheese gazetteer** . . . . . . . . . . . . . . . . . . . . . . . . . . . . . . . . . . .235

THANKS

If I were to mention everyone who had had a hand in the writing of this book, the list would include pretty much all my friends and colleagues, a number of over-stressed delivery drivers and the dogs of Southwark Park, and would take up more space than I have here. Thank you all. But I would like to single out for particular thanks the following:

As always, all the cheesemakers of Great Britain and Ireland and, in particular, those I managed to pin down and bombard with questions about their cheeses and backstories. Three of my fellow mongers, Wendy Barrie, Nick Bayne and Avril Molloy who pointed out my more egregious mistakes and omissions – any remaining ones are on me. Claire Littlejohn, who painted the mouth-watering pictures; Dominic Beddow, who created the enticing gazetteer; Nikky Twyman for proofreading; and Henry Iles, who tied the whole thing together. My editor Mark Ellingham, who does his best to make me appear succinct and comprehensible, and everyone at Profile Books for generally being marvellous. David Luxton, without whom my books would only exist on the backs of fag packets, and Rebecca Winfield for making sure I don't get into trouble for them. For rescuing me, fairly tirelessly, from The Pit of Writerly Despair, and for tasting an unfeasible number of cheeses – often at 7am – my best friend and my wife, Imogen Robertson.

# Introduction

Welcome to the *Cheesemonger's Compendium*! I hope you will find this a helpful aid to buying and enjoying some of the wonderful cheeses of Britain and Ireland. I am Ned Palmer, author of *A Cheesemonger's History of the British Isles* and for the last twenty years I have made my living looking after, selling and talking about cheese. As part of my job I've worked in cellars, on retail counters, hosted cheese tastings and travelled around the British Isles visiting farms and meeting cheesemakers. It is the most fun it is possible to have.

There are probably more than 1,500 individual cheeses in Britain and Ireland – a remarkable statistic, given that many of our traditional farmhouse cheeses were on the verge of extinction in the post-war years. That was a part of the story I told in the *Cheesemonger's History*. Here, my focus is very much on the cheeses themselves: how they taste, how they are made, and the often eccentric and colourful characters behind them – the cheesemakers and the *affineurs* (the mongers who turn and tend them to their perfect, matured state).

My own love affair with British cheese began on a chilly morning in December 2000 at Borough Market. I was there to help my friend Todd Trethowan sell his traditional farmhouse

Caerphilly, and of course the first thing I needed to do was to try some. It was not only the best cheese I'd ever had, but one of the most delicious and fascinating foods I'd ever eaten, delicate yet complex with a whole suite of flavours and textures. I won't describe them all here as you can look up the entry for Trethowan's Gorwydd Caerphilly to find out more. Tasting this cheese was a bit of a revelation for me – I'd never realised cheese could reach these heights of deliciousness and complexity. Also over the weeks that I worked on the stall with Todd I discovered how much there was to learn about cheese and cheesemaking, even through the medium of a single cheese, as with each delivery from his farm the cheeses looked and tasted different. I began to ask Todd questions, and a lot of them, so that before long he politely suggested that he might help me get a job at the famous cheese shop Neal's Yard Dairy, if I promised to stop bothering him.

Neal's Yard, or The Dairy as its alumni call it, specialises in farmhouse and artisan cheese from Great Britain and Ireland. The shop opened in the yard itself in London's Covent Garden in 1979 and at first sold yoghurt, ice-cream and fresh cheese that were all made on the premises. At that stage they didn't sell any other kinds of cheese, and given that Monty Python's office was in the same yard, it's tempting to think that the Dairy was the inspiration for the famous cheese sketch, except that the episode first aired in 1972, seven years before the shop opened. Then a fall in ice-cream and fresh cheese sales during the first winter persuaded Randolph Hodgson and Jane Scotter, the managers and later owners of the Dairy, that getting some more wintery cheeses in might be a good idea.

At first they sold the usual suspects: Cheddar, Stilton and Cheshire. Delivered by a wholesaler, these were all but anonymous, with no detail on who actually made the cheese, or where. The chance arrival of some farmhouse Caerphilly called Devon Garland, sent on spec by its maker, suggested that there might be more interesting cheeses and stories out there, and Randolph began scouring Britain and Ireland, visiting farms and dairies, and tracking down cheeses. By the time I arrived at the Dairy, more than twenty years later, there were more than fifty cheeses on the counter. For a young monger it was as if a new world had opened up before me. I hope, if you are not already a massive fan of British and Irish cheese, that reading this book will have a similar effect on you.

When I talk about the traditions of cheesemaking in these islands, you will notice that I only talk about British rather than British and Irish traditions. The reason for this is that, tragically, the vibrant culture of cheesemaking in Ireland was completely wiped out during the English conquest and colonisation of Ireland. Mere hints at what Irish cheese might have been like remain in some Irish words, for example, *tanag*, thought to be a hard skimmed milk cheese, and *faiscre grotha*, meaning 'pressed curd', which probably describes small cheeses pressed in moulds. But what with the climate and the lush grass, it was inevitable that cheesemaking would continue, and by the early twentieth century there was a flourishing Irish cheese industry. The cheeses were based on British styles and were at first known by their original names, as Irish Stilton or Irish Cheddar, but as success followed success – in 1936 Irish cheesemakers sold more than two and a half million pounds of cheese – these became known in their own right, named after the dairies that produced them, Ardagh, Galtee, Whitethorn to name but three.

Traditional British and Irish cheeses, however, had gone into decline in the post-war years, as factory farming and supermarkets squeezed out the old farmhouse producers. And then in the late 1970s came a Cheese Renaissance. This was in part a movement to save and to celebrate the last remaining traditional cheeses in Great Britain. At the same time, because so much traditional cheesemaking culture had been lost, people looked to Europe for inspiration and many of the cheeses of this renaissance are based on the traditional cheeses of France, Italy, Spain and Holland. Ireland, and more specifically County Cork, was one of the founts of this renaissance, where from around 1978 cheesemakers like Veronica Steele, Giana Ferguson and Jeffa Gill made washed-rind cheeses inspired by those of northern France. Not only did they make cheese, these were some of the founder members of CAIS, the Association of Irish Farmhouse Cheesemakers, which would itself be the inspiration for the British Specialist Cheesemakers Association, the SCA, set up in 1989. These days farmhouse and artisan cheese is flourishing in Ireland, and you will find many excellent examples in this book.

It's hard to know exactly how many different cheeses there are today in Britain and Ireland. New ones appear all the time, while sometimes cheesemakers retire, and if no one decides to take on the recipe, so does their cheese. Also, and I say this as a recovering philosopher, how do you count cheeses? Is Cheddar one cheese, or are Keen's, Hafod, St Andrews and Derg each a cheese unto themselves? I would say, conservatively, that there might be close to fifteen hundred British and Irish cheeses if you do count them all separately. Clearly I couldn't include them all in this compact volume. But the cheeses you will find in this book include all of my favourites, all of the best examples of their type, and some that are particularly interesting for one reason or another. Some of these I've known for years, even decades, and some I discovered for the first time writing this compendium.

You won't find any flavoured cheeses in here, that is to say the only ingredients will be milk, starter and ripening cultures, rennet and salt, and occasionally wood ash. This is not because

I am a fanatical cheese purist – I grew out of that last year when I discovered that the Romans enjoyed smoked and flavoured cheeses – but because when I am tasting cheese mindfully I want to taste the unflavoured cheese itself as an expression of the land it came from and the character of its maker.

The cheeses I have chosen are (nearly all) made by small scale producers using traditional methods. I describe these on the whole as either farmhouse or artisan cheeses, terms that need a bit of unpacking. By 'farmhouse', I mean cheeses that are made on the farm where the milk is produced, and these tend to be traditional styles like Cheddar, Red Leicester and Lancashire. A particular example might be Montgomery's Cheddar, made by the same family on their farm for over a century. I use 'artisan' to mean cheeses that are made with bought in milk and often not to traditional – or at least indigenous – recipes, although the methods are still traditional and the scale of production small. Mario Olianas' Yorkshire Pecorino, made in Leeds with local Yorkshire milk and Sardinian starter cultures, is an excellent example of the latter.

Of course there is some fuzziness in these categories: Coolea is made in Cork with the farm's own milk but to a Dutch recipe, and I am happy to call that farmhouse cheese. All Stilton is now made in creameries with bought-in milk rather than on farms, and has been since the 1930s, so by my definition it would be an artisan cheese, although it feels more like a farmhouse one to me, since it has been around for at least three hundred years and for most of that time was made on farms.

You will find both raw milk and pasteurised cheeses in this book. Raw, or unpasteurised, cheese is often prized because the individual character of the farm that produces it is expressed by the unique population of microflora in the milk, which would be killed by pasteurisation. The variation that so fascinated me in my early encounters with Gorwydd Caerphilly has a lot to do with how raw milk can change from day to day as these microflora change. However many excellent cheeses are made with pasteurised milk, including Coolea and Stilton, and both still show some variation across the seasons as the cows' diet and the weather change. I honestly find it difficult to imagine that either of them could be any more wonderful than they are.

The *Cheesemonger's Compendium* is divided into six colour-coded sections, each one representing what I call a family of cheese, **Fresh**, **Mould-ripened**, **Blue**, **Washed-rind**, **Semi-soft** and **Hard**. Such categorisations are open to dispute, of course, but that's cheesemongers for you. Within families, I also recognise particular styles, for example in the **Hard** family you will find the styles Cheddar, Red Leicester and Double Gloucester, and within the Blue family, Stilton and the Stilton styles, Stichelton, Young Buck and Sparkenhoe Blue.

At the end of the book, I've included some notes on how to buy cheese, and how to store it, how to taste cheese mind-fully, how to put together a cheeseboard and some ideas for matching cheese with drinks. If you have any cheese left over after all that, you will also find some ideas for cooking with cheese or turning it into spreads and dips.

You can find a list of **British and Irish cheesemongers** on my website, *www.cheesetastingco.uk* and many of these shops sell online. And if you're a cheesemaker, or enthusiast, I am always keen to hear about new cheeses, makers and mongers and indeed any musings or insights you may have about cheese. You can find me on Twitter at *@CheeseTastingCo*.

This book is dedicated to the cheesemakers.

# Fresh
# cheeses

# Fresh cheeses

Ballyhubbock Sheep's
Halloumi . . . . . . . . . . . . . . . . 18
Cote Hill White . . . . . . . . . . . 19
Clerkland Crowdie . . . . . . . . 20

Kedar Mozzarella . . . . . . . . . 21
Pant Ys Gawn . . . . . . . . . . . 22
Perroche. . . . . . . . . . . . . . . . 23
Yorkshire Fettle . . . . . . . . . . 24

# Fresh cheeses

I t seems right to open a celebration of the cheeses of Britain and Ireland with fresh cheeses, as the method for making them is the basis of production for all cheese – all the thousands of individual varieties, with their myriad differences of flavour, texture and appearance. Fresh cheese is the ur-cheese, dating back 9,000 years to Mesopotamia, and its creation required little more than a couple of bowls, a cloth or colander to drain curd, and a spoon to ladle it. Fresh cheese is also what you should try first on a cheeseboard, so as to be able to appreciate its delicate flavour. Once your palate has become acclimatised to the bold beefiness of a Cheddar or the piquancy of a Stilton, fresh cheeses can seem a little bland.

Let us see how it comes about. First, of course, you get your milk. To make really great cheese, you need high quality milk, and for that you need healthy happy animals. The best way to keep ruminant animals healthy and happy is to feed them their natural diet, which in the summer means the varied grasses and herbs of old pastures and, in the winter, hay and silage. Stressed animals do not give good milk, so it is as well to be nice to your livestock, particularly at milking time. And it means that merely by eating really good cheese you are encouraging sustainability and a concern for animal welfare, which is nice.

So now that you have this excellent milk, the first thing is to increase its acidity, or pickle it, rendering your milk inhospitable to any opportunistic spoilage bacteria. The most common way to do this is to add a dose of lactophilic bacteria to the milk. These helpful microorganisms consume the lactose so abundant in milk and convert it to lactic acid. Because this begins the process of cheesemaking, these bacteria are known as starter culture. (This is also, by the way, why the lactose intolerant can consume any variety of cheese that begins with this step – there is little or no remaining lactose in the cheese, as it is either converted or washed out with the whey.)

Next comes the drying step, which in cheesemaking means to coagulate your milk, separating the liquid whey from the solid curd. Actually, acidity has already begun this process and you could drain your acidified curd and be left with a very simple form of cheese (Indian Paneer, for example, is made by adding lemon juice rather than starter culture). To achieve a more through separation of liquid and solid, cheesemakers add rennet, an enzyme that encourages the milk protein casein to knit together in a matrix that captures the other solids in milk – the fats and minerals – separating them from the whey.

Rennet can be derived from the stomach of a calf or other ruminant animal, or it can have a vegetable origin, traditionally the sap of certain plants (the ancient Greeks and Romans used figs and some contemporary cheesemakers still use the cardoon thistle). Modern vegetarian rennet is derived from certain fungi or genetically modified *E. coli* bacteria.

The next step is to remove the whey, which for fresh cheeses is done by ladling the curds into moulds whose pierced bottoms let the liquid run out and also give shape to the cheeses. Once the cheeses have firmed up they are removed from the moulds and salted. The salt removes more moisture, adds a further protection against unwanted bacteria, and makes the cheese taste nice. Salt is clever.

Now that you know how to make cheese, let's talk about flavour. Intensity and complexity are largely the result of ageing; the starter bacteria die off relatively quickly and their cells break open to release enzymes that go to work developing flavour and texture. These are joined by a host of microbes – moulds, bacteria and yeasts – who all play their part in developing flavour. Fresh cheeses are eaten young when this motley yet well-disposed crew have not had much time to do their thing and so their flavours tend to be simple and more delicate. This is not to say that younger cheeses are bland or boring, it's just that more work is required of your palate.

Expect acidity in a soft cheese, an appropriately refreshing acidity but not the tingling bite of an aged Cheddar. Intertwined with and brought out by the acidity, there is a milky note, but not the mouth-filling creaminess of a ripe Camembert. There might be hints at other flavours, goatiness, a hint of almonds, something vegetal, but these are yet to blossom into their full expression. Much of the enjoyment of fresh cheeses is in their texture or mouthfeel, often moussey, even fluffy and just as satisfying an experience, when taken together with those characteristic flavours, as one might have with a more mature cheese.

# Ballyhubbock Sheep's Halloumi

## Made by George and Hanna Finlay in County Wicklow

🐑 PASTEURISED SHEEP'S MILK, ANIMAL RENNET

As a Halloumi-style cheese, Ballyhubbock is preserved in brine and lasts for ages, so it isn't exactly 'fresh'. Yet it is a rindless white cheese with a simple flavour so this still feels the right place for it. And, adding to the confusion, I've defined it above as a pasteurised cheese, which isn't exactly the case. The Finlays use raw milk but the temperature they need to heat the curd for their Halloumi means that it is in effect pasteurised.

For anyone who has only had plastic wrapped block Halloumi, this Irish version is a revelation – sweet, sheepy, with a slight note of honey and a loud squeak against your teeth when you chew it. Halloumi, with its high melting point, can be fried, or even barbecued, and these are great things to do with it. Ballyhubbock is so good I would eat it uncooked, on its own, until there was none left to cook.

George Finlay is the third generation of his family to farm this land, and had always wanted to set up a sheep dairying operation, so much so that at agricultural college he was named Sheep Student of the Year. It's nice when our dreams come true.

# Cote Hill White

## Made by the Davenport family in Lincolnshire

✖ UNPASTEURISED COW'S MILK, ANIMAL RENNET

The Davenports use milk from their own herd, which contains some Red Polls, a native breed which produces excellent milk and is descended from the extinct Suffolk Dun, once the powerhouse of East Anglian cheesemaking. Unpasteurised, and unruffled by a long commute, the milk is able to fully express its terroir – the cowslip on the Davenport's logo reflects the flavour that comes through in the milk when the cows have been grazing in a patch.

While most fresh cheeses have a moussy or fluffy texture, Cote Hill White feels more like a firm gel, the result of a rennet rather than lactic acid driven coagulation. The reason for this is eminently pragmatic as I found out when I spoke to Mary Davenport. With several different kinds of cheese to make, her son Joe doesn't want to wait for the twenty-four hours it would take for a lactic curd to set. Joe adds starter to the morning milk, still warm from the cow, and rennet just before lunch. The quick setting curd is ready to ladle by mid-afternoon. The firmer texture makes it an excellent ingredient in a green salad where its creaminess will make a lovely contrast to the freshness of the leaves.

# Clerkland Crowdie

## Made by Ann Dorward in Ayrshire

 PASTEURISED COW'S MILK, VEGETARIAN RENNET

Scottish cheese expert Wendy Barrie believes that Crowdie used to be made in farmhouse kitchens all over Scotland, once the cream had been skimmed off to make more lucrative butter. The milk soured naturally and was then heated – to set without rennet – then drained in muslin before being shaped into logs and rolled in oats. Ann Dorward, one of Wendy's favourite Crowdie producers, adds 'a tiny drop of rennet' for consistency's sake but the cheese is still just as I imagine her foremothers would have made, with a fresh creamy taste and a fluffy texture.

Scots eat Crowdie with scones and jam like a sort of edgy clotted cream, and as a protective measure before drinking whisky, a health benefit for cheese I've never come across before, but can heartily endorse.

Crowdie also features in my favourite cheese fairytale, a story from the Hebrides called 'Deer Dreaming' in which an old couple make Crowdie from deer milk and shape it into figures, which, coloured by the rays of the setting sun, fly out into the world to become the dreams, good and bad, true and false, dreamt by sleepers all over the world. So there you go, cheese does give you dreams.

# Kedar Mozzarella

## Made by Gavin and Jane Lochhead in Dumfries and Galloway

PASTEURISED COW'S MILK, VEGETARIAN RENNET

Mozzarella tends to be a more snowy white than other cow's milk cheeses. Kedar, however, is an enticingly creamy shade because the Lochheads' herd are Brown Swiss cows, famous for their hardiness, easy temper and the quality of their milk. For the breed geeks out there, Brown Swiss  are thought to be the oldest dairying cow, bred by the cheesemaking monks of Einsiedeln Abbey in Switzerland in the fifteenth century.

Despite that creamy appearance, Kedar has a very clean fresh flavour with just a gentle hint of cow and the excitingly stretchy texture characteristic of Mozzarella.

I have put this Mozzarella in the fresh cheese category because it is un-rinded, and should be eaten as young as possible while it retains that clean freshness. Actually, as a pasta fillata style, Mozzarella requires a bit more intervention than most fresh cheeses. The curd is heated to a blistering 77°C and then stretched and pulled, by pairs of cheesemakers standing at opposite sides of the dairy, great ropes of elastic curd stretching out between them so that they look like they are playing a skipping game.

# Pant Ys Gawn

## Made by the Craske family at Abergavenny, Gwent

 PASTEURISED GOAT'S MILK, VEGETARIAN RENNET

Pant Ys Gawn is made at a 40,000-square-foot facility on an industrial estate, which doesn't entirely fit with my preference for small-scale, rustic cheese making. The proof's in the eating, though. Its texture is very soft, like clotted cream, and the flavour is milky, developing a goaty tang surprising in a fresh cheese, and finishes with a particularly refreshing citrusy burst.

Also appealing is that Pant Ys Gawn, named for the farm where the family business began, is made without rennet – a truly ancient way of making cheese. This has its origin in a situation familiar to any small farmer over the last few thousand years, the need to find an alternative income stream. In the early 1980s, realising that arable wasn't viable, Pam and Tony Craske decided to give dairy farming a go. Tony went to the local market to buy a cow, and came back instead with six goats – which sounds like the beginning to a fairy tale. Soon oversupplied with milk, Pam got a book on cheesemaking from the local library and began making cheese.

Nowadays the Craskes buy in curd from local farms, all Soil Association accredited, so despite my reservations about scale this is a cheese that supports local producers and encourages organic farming. It's also very nice with strawberry jam.

# Perroche

## Made by Charlie Westhead and his team in Herefordshire

PASTEURISED GOAT'S MILK, ANIMAL RENNET

This cheese has everything you would expect in a fresh goat's cheese – rindless and snowy white, it has a soft fluffy texture, zingy acidity and only the merest goaty tang. Goatiness can be a problem for some people and even put them off goat's cheese for life, which is a shame. Young cheeses have little if any goatiness; the flavour becomes more pronounced as fatty acids responsible for it breakdown during ripening. These by the way are called capric, caproic and caprylic acid – all from the same root, *capra*, the Latin for 'goat'. So the goat-shy could stick to younger cheeses, or choose older cheeses made with gentleness and patience – two key skills for cheesemaking. The ungentle and impatient cheesemaker stirring the milk vigorously, or heating it too fast, will break down the fatty acids releasing their aromas more thoroughly.

I happen to like the goaty flavour, but this doesn't mean that I want my cheese to taste of nothing but – good cheese isn't just complex, it is balanced. In this case the goaty flavour has its role to play within an orchestra of flavours (including a hint of almond in the finish). Perroche, which sounds like a French cheese name, is actually a portmanteau of its inventors' names: Perry James and Beatrice Garroche.

# Yorkshire Fettle

## Made by the Bell family in Yorkshire

PASTEURISED SHEEP'S MILK, ANIMAL RENNET

'Fettle' is a Yorkshire dialect word that means, among other things, 'to be in good condition'. Which suits this cheese. Greek Feta is often a mix of goat and sheep's milk, and can

be pretty pungent, whereas Fettle is clean with a slightly bouncy texture – a bit like Halloumi – and given its firmness could also happily be fried or grilled. The cheese has balanced salt, a sweet milky flavour with a hint of biscuit dough and is pleasingly acidic.

The Bells originally called their wax-covered cheese Feta but had to change the name under pressure from Greek producers. At the beginning of the Covid crisis in Britain, a precipitous drop in demand threatened to destroy sheep dairying in Britain, and the Bells decided to relaunch Fettle as a fresh, unwaxed cheese under the slogan 'Save Our Sheep Milk' to provide an outlet for the milk and bring attention to the plight of the producers. They had none of the kit or systems in place to make and roll out the cheese, but according to Caroline Bell 'everyone dug in', and they went from a standing start to distribution in five months. It is fitting then that 'fettle' itself came from a Middle English word meaning 'to make ready for battle'.

# Mould-ripened cheeses

# Mould-ripened cheeses

Ailsa Craig . . . . . . . . . . . . . . . 33
Angiddy . . . . . . . . . . . . . . . . 34
Baron Bigod . . . . . . . . . . . . . 35
Bix . . . . . . . . . . . . . . . . . . . . . 36
Brefu Bach . . . . . . . . . . . . . . . 37
Cavanbert . . . . . . . . . . . . . . . 38
Cenarth Brie . . . . . . . . . . . . . 39
Corleggy Kid . . . . . . . . . . . . . 40
Dorstone . . . . . . . . . . . . . . . . 41
Elmhirst . . . . . . . . . . . . . . . . . 42
Elrick Log . . . . . . . . . . . . . . . 43
Flower Marie . . . . . . . . . . . . . 44
Golden Cross . . . . . . . . . . . . . 45
Hebden . . . . . . . . . . . . . . . . . 46
Little She . . . . . . . . . . . . . . . . 47
Lord London . . . . . . . . . . . . . 48
Ragstone . . . . . . . . . . . . . . . . 49
Saint George . . . . . . . . . . . . . 50
Saint Jude . . . . . . . . . . . . . . . 51
Saint Tola . . . . . . . . . . . . . . . 52
Saint Tola Ash . . . . . . . . . . . . 53
Sinodun Hill . . . . . . . . . . . . . 54
The Cheese With No Name . . . 55
Tor . . . . . . . . . . . . . . . . . . . . . 56
Triple Rose . . . . . . . . . . . . . . . 57
Tunworth . . . . . . . . . . . . . . . . 58
Wicklow Bán . . . . . . . . . . . . . 59
Wigmore . . . . . . . . . . . . . . . . 60
Winslade . . . . . . . . . . . . . . . . 61
Witheridge . . . . . . . . . . . . . . . 62

# Mould-ripened cheeses

Brie and Camembert are the best known members of this family and plenty of fine examples of these classic French cheeses are made in Britain and Ireland, like the Camembert-style Tunworth or the Brie-style Wicklow Ban. But the very fact that we define them by their French cousins suggest that this is not, or at least not thought to be, a traditional style in either country.

By their rinds shall you know them and mould-ripened cheeses are usually edged with the white or grey of *Penicillium camemberti* and *Geotrichum candidum* (henceforth *P. camemberti* and *Geo.*). They are creamier, more intense and more complex than their younger cousins, the fresh cheeses, and this is the result of the action of the rind on the paste.

The method for making a mould-ripened cheese is much the same as for a fresh one. You sour and set the milk with starter culture and rennet, ladle the set curd into moulds, let the whey drain off, and turn out the young cheeses. Many mould-ripened cheeses – goat's milk styles like Sinodun Hill from Oxfordshire or Black Mount from Lanarkshire – are slow-setting lactic styles, where coagulation is driven more by the lactic acid produced by starter culture than by rennet. The curd can take up to twenty-four hours to set, and is not cut before ladling into moulds. For other styles like Camembert, the milk is gently heated and more rennet is used so that the curd sets in a fraction of the time – as little as an hour – and the curd is cut before ladling to help more whey to drain off.

The most significant difference is that, while you could eat your fresh cheeses there and then, mould-ripened cheeses need a few weeks in a cool moist place – a cellar or cave – to grow their coats of mould and ripen into something creamier and more complex. Traditionally the moulds would be whatever species or strains were indigenous to your cellar, giving each cheese-maker's cheese a unique character. Modern cheesemakers often use bought mould cultures, which are added to the milk in the first stage of making, or sprayed onto young cheeses while they mature, giving more predictable and consistent outcomes. However, some cheesemakers still allow nature to take its course by adding no extraneous moulds, while others follow a middle way, adding some bought cultures to the cheese, often in the earlier part of the making season, but leaving room for naturally occurring moulds to develop alongside.

It's likely that this family first appeared in the early medieval period, when peasant cheesemakers used the Roman method for soft cheesemaking outlined in Columella's *De re rustica* – essentially the process described above – in the cool damp climate of northern France. The soft fresh cheeses that would have to be eaten fast in the warmer climate of southern Europe could be kept for longer, and developed these interesting rinds and richer and more complex flavours. This minimal intervention, low-tech recipe, with its long pauses, would have been ideal for the busy cheesemaker in a peasant household.

Cheesemaking fell to the women in this society, who also made bread, beer and yarn, and looked after children, pigs and chickens. These and many other tasks could be fitted in around the cheesemaking regime when, for example, the curd needed to set or the cheeses drain in their moulds. There was another factor which led to the appearance of these cheeses, which is that peasants don't tend to own very many animals. It wouldn't have been worth making cheese with the small amount you'd get from one day's milking of a single cow, and so these cheesemakers probably kept milk over a few days until there was enough to be getting on with, and without refrigeration the milk would have soured naturally, creating a higher acid curd that favoured the development of moulds.

Mould-ripened cheeses get their complex characters from the action of various microorganisms on the fats and proteins in the curd, but then (apart from the fresh cheeses) this is the same for all cheeses, so we ought to clear up some terminology. For nearly all the blue cheeses, this happens within the paste rather than on the surface (another name for that family is internally ripened). Both mould-ripened and washed-rind cheeses ripen from the outside, so both families are members of a larger category called surface-ripened. However, for washed-rinds the predominant ripening organisms are bacteria rather than moulds, so they have their own separate section. If we were going to be really proper about it, we could describe the family of cheeses in this section as surface-mould-ripened, which is a bit of a mouthful. If you say mould-ripened to a cheesemonger or maker, they'll know what you're talking about.

Ripening is a fantastically complex process. The moulds, yeasts and bacteria are not mere ingredients of flavour – it is their action on the proteins and fats in the cheese that create flavour; furthermore these various microorganisms interact with each other and in doing so their activity and the products of that activity also change. But this is not all! The aromatic compounds which are products of ripening give flavour and themselves interact with each other, and are precursors for other aromatic compounds, with their own flavours and interactions which in turn are precursors for more aromatic compounds. It's no wonder that cheese is so exciting!

Broadly speaking, ripening involves two processes: *proteolysis*, the breakdown of protein into amino acids, giving the sweet, sour, bitter and umami flavours; and more importantly in mould-ripened cheese, *lipolysis*, the breakdown of lipids like fats, oils and the vitamins A, D, E and K into various aromatic compounds. The earliest products of this ripening process are fatty acids, in particular the volatile short chain ones, which have a lower perception threshold, so we are more likely to notice their aromatic contribution. One of the most prevalent in cheese is butyric acid, which contributes a buttery note as well as (less informatively) a cheesy one. Butyric acid can also contribute notes of old socks and baby sick – which might sound unpleasant, but when imperceptibly intertwined in a whole palette of flavours they add complexity. (Parmesan is well supplied with butyric acid, and is one of the most popular cheeses in the world, although some people can't stand it and tend to accuse it of tasting like baby sick.) The 'goaty' flavours in goat's milk come from a collection of short chain fatty acids called caproic, caprylic and capric – essentially Latinate variations on 'goaty'.

Between them, those busy little moulds *Geo.* and *P. camemberti* also produce ketones, methyl ketones, alcohols, lactones, esters, aldehydes and, through proteolysis, sulphur compounds. If the latter category doesn't sound all that appetising, it probably won't help to know that both moulds are keen producers of methanethiol, which is the substance added to natural gas to give it a warning aroma, and can literally, like some cheeses I have known, clear a room. The thing is that this and other sulphur compounds found in cheese have aromas which can include cooked cauliflower, cabbage, onions and garlic, all of which can be found in a deliciously ripe mould-ripened cheese, like Tunworth. They also show a 'cheesy' aroma and (I'm not quite so enthusiastic about this) an occasional note of 'crab' – a flavour note that can add an interesting edge to a cheese, like a Thai fish sauce. As for the alcohols, there are so many to be found in cheese that I'm not sure why we bother drinking wine with it. 2-heptanol produces an earthy aroma, and the catchily named 1-Octen-3-ol smells of mushrooms, both of which are favourite mould-ripened notes of mine.

Using its proteolytic superpower, *P. camemberti* breaks amino acids into peptides, which have a bitter flavour, and if you see a cheese with a pure white unwrinkled rind largely formed from that mould, the chances are there will be some bitterness in the flavour. Happily, *Geo.* is an enthusiastic liberator of oleic acid, which as a medium chain acid makes little contribution to flavour except that it masks bitterness. *Geo.* tends to be greyish and wrinkly, so if you have a low threshold for bitterness, as I do, you might prefer cheeses with a less white and more uneven-looking rind. This is only one of a myriad of ways that different microorganisms collaborate to create and manage flavours.

Appearance is important in a cheese, and a less uniformly coloured and textured rind suggests complexity. As well as controlling bitterness, *Geo.* adds vegetal and sulphurous notes, and I am particularly excited if I see some flecks of pinkish brown announcing the presence of the bacteria *Brevibacterium linens* which, prevalent in washed-rinds, adds a little funk to the mix in a mould-ripened cheese. On some goat's cheeses you will see a grey or even black layer peeping through the lighter colours;

this is the wood ash that is dusted onto some varieties. Originally added to keep off flies, the ash seems to lower the acidity of the cheese, making it more hospitable for some strains of mould.

As well as creating flavour, the moulds affect the texture of the cheese through their activity, changing the firm white paste of a young cheese into the softer creamier colour of an older one. All this activity is going on at the surface and moving from there into the paste and so this manifests as a creamy layer between the rind and the centre of the cheese called the *breakdown*. Its depth tells you how ripe the cheese is. This is a useful visual aid for the cheese-buying public, and as with so many aspects of cheese is very much a personal thing. Many people are excited by extremely ripe cheeses: 'Look! It's running away!' is an enthusiastic cry often heard at the cheese counter just before someone, to the monger's immense relief, buys an entire worryingly-ripe Brie. If you prefer milder flavours you might prefer to see less breakdown in your cheese, and even a paler chalky stripe running down the middle. This layer will have a lighter citrusy flavour and firmer texture and makes a very pleasant contrast to the creamy breakdown. The French call it *l'âme de fromage*, meaning 'the soul of the cheese', which is my favourite cheese fact.

As well as sight, aroma can tell us how far a cheese is along its own individual ripening journey. Ammonia is the ultimate breakdown product of the amino group, so the higher the level of it you can smell in your cheese, the riper it is. At the optimal point, you might just sense its presence among the rich panoply of flavours; in an end-stage cheese you might be hit with an eye-watering whiff of ammonia and, as much as I value balance in a cheese, sometimes that's rather fun.

# Ailsa Craig

## Made by Ann Dorward in Ayrshire

PASTEURISED GOAT'S MILK, VEGETARIAN RENNET

With its rounded shape and knobbly texture, this striking cheese looks like its namesake, the rocky volcanic island out in the Firth of Clyde also known as Paddy's Milestone for its position in the Irish sea, a landmark for Irish labourers sailing to Britain to look for work. The wrinkly *Geotrichum* texture is well covered with a snowy white layer of *Penicillium camemberti* such that Ailsa Craig also looks like a small white cloud. Its aroma is milky and mushroomy and the texture, carrying on the cloudy theme, is delightfully light and fluffy. The domination of the *camemberti*, which for once I celebrate, gives a very clean flavour – I can't detect any sulphurous notes from the *Geo.* – with only a hint of goat, a little earthiness topped off with a lemon finish and well-balanced salt.

If I wanted to encourage the novice goat fancier to make the leap from fresh to mould-ripened cheeses, Ailsa Craig would be a great one to start with. Ann also makes a small fresh cow's milk cheese called Paddy's Milestone and I think these two would make great partners on a cheeseboard.

# Angiddy

## Made at Brooke's Dairy in Monmouthshire

🐄 PASTEURISED COW'S MILK, VEGETARIAN RENNET

What I love about cheese is that whenever I come up with a rule, like 'good mould-ripened cheeses have wrinkly multi-coloured rinds', an exception pops up.

Angiddy is one of these, Its smooth white rind is all *Penicillium camemberti*, with not a trace of *Geotrichum* or any other microorganism to be seen. The rind has an aroma of fresh paper, and the texture is quite firm with little sign of breakdown – often a sign of an immature cheese, though in this case I think it denotes slow and gentle ripening. The paste is the warm golden colour of Jersey milk and has an aroma of hay, and a clean flavour like fresh cream, finishing on a green herb note. There are none of the vegetal or sulphurous notes *Geotrichum* tends to contribute, and this cheese pleases me for its simplicity rather than its complexity. Often pure *Penicillium camemberti* rinds tend towards bitterness; that there is none in this cheese speaks of skilful cheesemaking and *affinage*.

The Brookes of Monmouthshire have always used their Jersey milk to make ice-cream, which is clearly a great preparation for cheesemaking. Angiddy won a gold medal in the World Cheese Awards of 2017 only months after its creation.

# Baron Bigod

## Made by Jonny Crickmore and his team in Norfolk

UNPASTEURISED COW'S MILK, ANIMAL RENNET

An English take on Brie, Baron Bigod is named after a Norman lord of the manor and has all the depth and complexity you would expect from a style that was declared the king of cheeses at the Congress of Vienna in 1815. The wrinkled rind with its flecks of orange and golden brown denote the presence of moulds and yeasts that contribute flavours reminiscent of the *Brassica* genus of vegetables, which include cauliflower, cabbage and broccoli and which are also known as mustard plants.

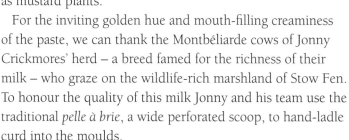

For the inviting golden hue and mouth-filling creaminess of the paste, we can thank the Montbéliarde cows of Jonny Crickmores' herd – a breed famed for the richness of their milk – who graze on the wildlife-rich marshland of Stow Fen. To honour the quality of this milk Jonny and his team use the traditional *pelle à brie*, a wide perforated scoop, to hand-ladle curd into the moulds.

Somewhat fatter than a Brie, Baron Bigod often retains a pale chalky stripe through the centre of the paste. Far from a fault, this provides a contrasting texture and flavour to the softer yellow edge. As noted earlier, the French call this *l'âme de fromage* – the soul of the cheese.

# Bix

## Made by Rose Grimond and her team in Oxfordshire

PASTEURISED COW'S MILK, ANIMAL RENNET

Before making cheese, Rose Grimond ran a stall at Borough Market, and before that she was an actor, thus completing the trifecta of excellent ways to not make a fortune. I have a lot of sympathy with this career path, having moved from the theatre to a stall at Borough Market and then into cheese, but there the similarity ends. Rose is a far more accomplished cheesemaker than I will ever be, and has a much finer pedigree, being among other things Celia Johnson's granddaughter and Ian Fleming's great-niece – the James Bond author's grandfather bought the Nettlebed estate, where Bix is made, in 1903.

Rose's family decided to start cheesemaking in 2012 when selling their high quality organic milk to Dairy Crest stopped being economically viable. Now, if you're going to add value to your milk by making cheese, you may as well add as much value as possible, and this luxuriant *triple-crème* style, made with added double cream, fits the bill. The colour is very deep yellow, like Jersey butter, and the texture has the richness of Devon clotted cream; the flavour is clean with a mineral edge and a hint of mushrooms from the rind.

# Brefu Bach

## Made by Carrie Rimes in Gwynedd

🐑 UNPASTEURISED SHEEP'S MILK, ANIMAL RENNET

Like many sheep's cheeses, Brefu Bach is startlingly sweet – its luxuriant silky texture reminds me of vanilla ice-cream – though the wrinkly *Geotrichum* rind adds savoury vegetal flavours to remind you that you are actually eating cheese. That creamy texture is down to the high fat content of sheep's milk (which can be almost twice that of cow's), a texture retained by Carrie's gentle cheesemaking process. The complex flavour, with a floral note, nuttiness and a hint of caramel, shows the benefit of grazing on old leys – fields with a richly multicultural population of grasses, herbs and legumes, on which these native Lleyn sheep are born to thrive.

Carrie's background is as diverse as these pastures, and also contributes to the excellent quality of her cheese. She grew up on a West Country dairy farm, although being in Devon her family made clotted cream rather than cheese. Dismayed at the loss of old pastures to modern farming methods, she originally worked as a grassland research scientist and her profound knowledge and infectious enthusiasm for traditional  pasture shines through. For those readers whose Welsh is a little rusty, *Brefu Bach* means 'Little Bleat'.

# Cavanbert

## Made by Silke and Tom Cropp in County Cavan

🐄 UNPASTEURISED COW'S MILK, ANIMAL RENNET

The snow-white rind of this cheekily named cheese suggests the dominance of *Penicillium camemberti*, and while there is a wrinkle of *Geotrichum* the mostly smooth surface and uniform colour tells you that simplicity and restraint will characterise its flavour profile. The aroma is milky with just a tinge of ammonia, with minimal breakdown and a firm but pleasingly moist centre. Up front, the flavour is clean with a definite mineral edge, finishing on a note of fresh uncooked cabbage.

Silke and her husband came over to Ireland from Germany in 1985, bought a smallholding complete with a fairy tale tumbledown cottage, and a 'semi-wild' goat for their milk. In a familiar plot twist, there proved to be too much goat's milk to drink and so Silke began making cheese in the kitchen with recipes from an old book and some cut-down drainpipes for moulds. Her original cheese was the hard goat's milk Corleggy, and soft cow's cheese is a recent development. Clearly this was a great place to start – Cavanbert is the most sessionable Camembert style I've come across and it took an effort to stop eating the cheese and start writing.

# Cenarth Brie

## Made by the Adams family in Carmarthenshire

 PASTEURISED COW'S MILK, VEGETARIAN RENNET

A strong candidate for best-named cheesemakers in Britain, the Adams family have a cheese ancestry dating back to 1903. With that frugal spirit common to farmers, Thelma Adams' father originally bored holes in old corned-beef tins to make moulds for her mother's farmhouse Caerphilly. Things stepped up a gear, however, in 1984, when the UK government's ham-fisted implementation of EU milk quotas meant farmers might be forced to throw away surplus milk, or reduce the size of their herds. As a protest, Thelma dressed as Cleopatra and, with ten other women, took a bath in milk on the streets of Carmarthen, bringing the town to a standstill. A few years later she restarted cheesemaking on the family farm to address the surplus.

Like Angiddy, Cenarth Brie has a pure white rind, though I discern the merest wrinkle of *Geotrichum*. The paste is thoroughly broken down, giving a lovely rich liquid texture, and the flavour is mild for such a ripe cheese, with just a trace of cabbage and, in the finish, a sulphuric note like the yolk of a boiled egg.

# Corleggy Kid

## Made by Silke and Tom Cropp in County Cavan

🐾 UNPASTEURISED GOAT'S MILK, VEGETARIAN RENNET

I was sent a sample of this young cheese that was perhaps three days old, showing only scant traces of *Penicillium candidum* on the surface. Consequently the texture was firm, slightly chalky, and squeaked against my teeth in a way reminiscent of Halloumi. The acidity was so low that the predominant flavour was of just-soured milk, with a slight tang of goat. I really enjoyed these gentle flavours and the firm texture, unlike any I've seen in an ostensibly mould-ripened cheese, but I wondered if this was deliberate. Unsure, I rang Sheridans cheesemonger Quentin Duboz, who said that Silke and Tom do like their cheese at this age. Quentin is from the Jura in France and, true to his origin, likes to mature the cheeses in his shop until they more resemble a French style.

This illustrates an aspect of the relationship between maker and *affineur* like that between a musician and a record producer, where both have creative input into the finished product. With the firm younger cheese, like Corleggy Kid, Quentin recommends an enticing snack – two slices of the Kid, with a spoonful of fig compote and a thin slice of Iberico ham on a piece of soda bread, gently warmed in the oven. I'm off to try it now.

# Dorstone

## Made by Charlie Westhead and his team in Herefordshire

🐐 PASTEURISED GOAT'S MILK, ANIMAL RENNET

I love Dorstone, particularly when it is young and the paste is so open and fluffy and the acidity so bright and zesty that it's a bit like consuming cheesy sherbet. This marvellous texture is to some extent the result of a particular technique that sets Dorstone apart from Charlie Westhead's other cheeses (see Perroche and Ragstone). After twenty-four hours of souring and setting, the curd for the other cheeses is ladled into moulds and begins to drain. For Dorstone the curd is ladled onto a table, to pre-drain before it is moulded. Paradoxically, the increased loss of moisture at this stage means you end up with a more open fluffier texture later on. Cheese is magic like that.

The acidity in Dorstone does a lovely job of bringing out the fruit in other products. For this reason I am keen on pairing the cheese with raspberry jam. Similarly it would be nice to drink something jammy like a Beaujolais or a red Labrusco with Dorstone, or you could really go for the whole sherbet experience and break out the bubbly.

# Elmhirst

## Made by Debbie Mumford and her team in Devon

UNPASTEURISED COW'S MILK, ANIMAL RENNET

For all us cheese geeks, here's something rather special: a cheese sub-sub-category. Not only is Elmhirst a soft cheese, and within that, a mould-ripened cheese, but it is also a *triple-crème*, which distinguishes this positively sybaritic offering from similar mould-ripened cheeses like Camembert or Brie.

To make a *triple-crème*, you get your already rich full-cream milk and add extra cream to it. Only the French would think of doing such a thing. The texture is opulent, like slightly edgy clotted cream, and rewards pairing with a sparkling wine, which is lucky because several rather smashing ones are also made on the Sharpham estate: what grows together often goes together.

Where Elmhirst differs from more peppery and vegetal mould-ripened cheeses like Camembert and Brie is the cleanness and simplicity of its flavour. Counter-intuitively for a cheese, eating this makes me think of drinking water fresh from a mountain spring after a long hot climb.

# Elrick Log

## Made by Angela Cairns and the Erringtons in Lanarkshire

UNPASTEURISED GOAT'S MILK, ANIMAL RENNET

Although it may sound like a Michael Moorcock hero, Elrick Log is actually named after an old spelling of Elsrickle, a village just over the hill from the Erringtons' farm.

The geographical naming of cheese is an ancient practice. Territorials are either named for their counties, like Gloucestershire, or Lancashire, or for the markets where they were sold, like Caerphilly and Cheddar. More specifically, the Erringtons name some of their cheeses for local features like the Black Mount and Tinto hills, a practice I can imagine stretching back to the Neolithic origins of cheesemaking. When ancient farmers arrived in the British Isles, they brought their goats with them, whose feral descendants live wild and free in Northumberland and over the sea in County Kerry – goat's cheesemaking in these islands also has an ancient past.

This cheese is as complex and interesting as you would hope from one with a pedigree stretching back thousands of years, with a delicate fungal and milky aroma and a melt in the mouth texture. A light goatiness is enhanced by a peppery note from the rind and brightened with a lemony finish.

# Flower Marie

## Made by Kevin and Alison Blunt in Sussex

 UNPASTEURISED SHEEP'S MILK, ANIMAL RENNET

Pretty in name and appearance, Flower Marie comes in snow-white pillowy little cubes three inches across. There is a floral delicacy to their flavour, which also shows hints of mushrooms, and a hint of acidity. When young, the paste has the texture of firm ice-cream, but with age develops a richer line of breakdown under the rind, the flavour becoming more intense and more fatty with a hint of sheepy lanolin.

The name is a sort of anglicised version of *Fleur de Maquis*, which is funny because those Corsican cheeses have a much more rustic look, with their rough covering of herbs from the dense scrubland that covers the island of Corsica. This continental inspiration was typical of cheeses developed in the British Cheese Renaissance and Flower Marie was developed by one of the heroes of that movement – cheesemonger and maker James Aldridge – and named for the late Ann-Marie Dyas, who set up the Fine Cheese Company in Bath in 1995. In the early 1990s, Aldridge taught Kevin and Alison Blunt how to make the cheese, showing a generosity of spirit that belied his tough exterior. Cheesemongers are nice, when you get to know them.

# Golden Cross

## Made by Kevin and Alison Blunt in Sussex

UNPASTEURISED GOAT'S MILK, ANIMAL RENNET

It is fascinating how cheeses made from the same ingredients and to broadly the same method can be so different. It's one thing to see that in a Cheddar versus a washed-rind, but it's pretty amazing to find considerable differences between a much narrower category: two English goat's cheese logs. Merely looking at a Golden Cross compared to, say, a Ragstone is instructive.

Golden Cross has a smooth uniformly white rind compared to Ragstone's rather rumpled coat. This indicates, in the former, the domination of the mould *Penicillium candidum*, and while I am often a fan of more multicultural rinds, with a mix of different moulds and yeasts, in this case the simple flavour and texture of the rind allows one to focus on the flavour of the cheese, in which, again unlike Ragstone, there is a pronounced nutty flavour, specifically hazelnut. Patches of black may show through, a sign that this cheese has been coated in ash, which, being an alkaline substance, appears to lower the acidity of the cheese. Where the paste of a Ragstone has an open fluffy texture, that of a Golden Cross is dense and firm, and this texture coats the mouth sensuously.

# Hebden

## Made by Gillian Clough in West Yorkshire

🐐 UNPASTEURISED GOAT'S MILK, ANIMAL RENNET

Gillian Clough – whose day job is radiography lecturer – came to the world of cheesemaking through a fondness for goats, particularly Anglo-Nubians, which happen to give excellent milk. She bought ten to rear on a small farm in the Pennines, and it was only when she and her husband found themselves with a surfeit of milk that she began cheesemaking, starting with a fresh cheese called Gat, old English for 'goat'. Andy Swinscoe, owner of the Courtyard Dairy, was so impressed with the quality of their milk that he suggested that Gillian try making something more complex, and Hebden was born – the result of close collaboration between the two.

Hebdens come in small plump discs with a ramified wrinkly surface indicating the predominance of the yeasty mould *Geotrichum* and a dark cream colour. The texture is fudgey with very little breakdown and an intriguing aroma that combines honey with a tart, salty note evoking the seaside. A skein of goatiness is elegantly woven into a palate of flavours that includes straw, honey and fresh yeast, all tied up in an exciting peppery finish.

# Little She

## Made by Roger Longman and his team in Somerset

🐑 UNPASTEURISED SHEEP'S MILK, VEGETARIAN RENNET

These plump little discs have a snowy white coat of *Penicillium candidum* with a light wrinkle of *Geotrichum*. The rind has a light papery aroma with a hint of cellar, with caramel and citrus from the paste. This rind is paper thin, with little breakdown underneath, and the paste is springy with a dusting of small holes. This texture and the sweet low-acid flavour would suggest a washed-curd except that their maker, Roger Longman, doesn't hold with that technique, preferring to keep the acidity low from the start. The flavour is gentle with a malty caramel note, a hint of lanolin, and a citric tang.

At present Roger makes a barely believable twenty cheese varieties, with a team of three cheesemakers and an approach he calls 'chaos theory'. Actually the method is more intentional and more elegant. On Monday, starting with a single vat, they make twelve different cheeses, beginning with soft Brie styles, whose curd is ready for the moulds in three hours. An hour later the hard cheeses are draining, and in the afternoon the rest of the milk has been started and renneted and will sit overnight to be made into slow-setting lactic cheeses the next day. 'We like a challenge,' he says laconically.

# Lord London

## Made by Arthur Alsop in Sussex

🐾 PASTEURISED COW'S MILK, ANIMAL RENNET

The bell-like shape of Lord London is similar to a Spanish cheese called Tetilla, Galician for 'small breast'. This cheese's less anatomical name commemorates the 2012 Olympics which it was created to celebrate. It was also served at Prince William and Princess Kate's wedding breakfast, which shows that they (or at least their wedding planners) have excellent taste in cheese.

Unlike the Spanish cheese's waxy coating, Lord London has a mould rind which, consisting of a paper-thin coat of pure *Penicillium camemberti*, doesn't distract from the delicate simple flavours of the cheese. Inside the rind is a bright yellow paste with a uniform texture showing no breakdown and a scattering of propionic holes promising sweetness. The aroma is buttery, with a light tang of ammonia. The texture is springy, breaking down into creaminess in the mouth and delivering a warm buttery flavour with a tangy acidity and just a note of mossy earth. In response to the 2020 lockdown, Arthur changed the recipe for Lord London to make a firmer, longer-keeping cheese, which accounts for the gentle flavour and uniform texture. It's nice to think that someting so lovely can arise from adversity.

# Ragstone

## Made by Charlie Westhead and his team in Herefordshire

🐐 PASTEURISED GOAT'S MILK, ANIMAL RENNET

When young, Ragstones are like log-shaped fluffy white clouds and their flavour is simple: fresh and acidic. As they age, the white *Penicillium candidum*, rubbed and smoothed down by the *affineurs*, dies back and more of the wrinkly *Geotrichum* shows through. Everyone gets more complex as they age and cheese is no exception. Ragstones begin to display more vegetal flavours, the acidity falls, and sweeter nuttier flavours show through. The paste is much less dense than that of a Golden Cross but on the firm rather than moussey side.

Ragstone was the first cheese that Charlie Westhead created himself, when he took over Neal's Yard Creamery in 1990. It was actually developed in response to a shortage of Golden Cross, which was selling so well that the Blunts couldn't keep up with demand. I doubt that Charlie ever set out to directly copy the Blunts' cheese, because that would be boring and wrong and also impossible. Even if you attempted to reproduce every aspect of the Golden Cross recipe, you would end up with something new. The beauty of cheesemaking is that it's not reducible to recipes or algorithms.

# Saint George

## Made by Lyn and Jenny Jenner in Sussex

PASTEURISED GOAT'S MILK, VEGETARIAN RENNET

Saint George has a good balance of pure white *Penicillium* to a wrinkly underlay of *Geotrichum*. The young cheeses, before those moulds have really got to work, have a fairly firm paste with little breakdown. The flavours are mild, with only a hint of goat and retain a fresh acidity. Older cheeses have a more creamy yellow colour to the rind, with more *Geotrichum*, a liquid paste and a sharp whiff of ammonia. Cabbaginess has appeared, along with a pronounced goaty flavour and a peppery heat in the finish. As with all mould-ripened cheeses, you could take your Saint George on this ripening journey yourself, if you kept the cheese in its waxed paper wrapping in the salad drawer of your fridge for a week or two.

The Jenners began making cheese on their Sussex farm in 1979, putting them among the pioneers of the Cheese Renaissance. They originally bought a goat for its milk because their dog kept barking at the milkman in the morning and it was upsetting the neighbours. Goats are sociable creatures, and one on its own would have been sad, so the Jenners bought a few companions and, with all the milk that started appearing, realised they would have to turn it into cheese.

# Saint Jude

## Made by Julie Cheyney in Suffolk

UNPASTEURISED COW'S MILK, VEGETABLE RENNET

Saint Jude is another cheese that you can take on a rewarding journey. When young, it has a firm texture as the rind has had less chance to soften the paste, and for the same reason the flavour is delicate and clean. I would recommend pairing it with a sparkling wine for a wonderful

combination of sparkle and fudgey mousse in the mouth. If that wine has an element of toasted brioche so much the better, like a sort of boozy scone and clotted cream experience.

Older Saint Judes soften to the point of liquidity and develop brassic and farmyardy flavours – nothing untoward, just a gentle hint of the byre. Even when aged, this is a still a cheese with a sense of propriety; I've never had one display that ammoniac sting behind the eyes that an elderly Camembert can inflict.

Many cheeses are named for saints – a millennia-old connection between cheese and the supernatural and perhaps an attempt to enlist godly help in the chancy business of cheesemaking. Julie Cheyney had already been a partner in one cheesemaking start up when she decided to strike out on her own, which is perhaps that's why this cheese is named for the patron saint of lost causes, Saint Jude.

# Saint Tola

## Made by Siobhán Ni Ghairbhith and her team in County Clare

🐐 UNPASTEURISED GOAT'S MILK, ANIMAL RENNET

Saint Tola has a rind the colour of the crust on clotted cream and a thick wavy wrinkle of *Geotrichum*. Rinds with a thick coat of that yeasty mould can often be quite wet and tend to slip off the cheese and it shows skilful cheesemaking and *affinage* that this one is pleasantly moist and remains firmly attached to the paste. The aroma is yoghurty with a hint of yeast and a fresh green savoury herbal note like chives. The thick moussey texture is lifted with a lemony acidity with a mere memory of goatiness well integrated into the flavour, The rind adds a light earthiness and clean vegetal note with none of the more funky elements that *Geotrichum* can confer.

The cheese is named for a seventh-century saint who founded a monastic community in northwestern Clare, and whose crozier, the symbol of his pastoral care for his flock, can be seen in the National Museum of Ireland. The early monasteries of Ireland were not only repositories of learning in chaotic post-Roman Europe but also of cheesemaking. Like many Irish prelates, Tola sent Irish missionaries to the continent, where according to some Irish cheesemakers they not only spread the Word but taught the pagans how to make cheese.

# Saint Tola Ash

## Made by Siobhán Ni Ghairbhith and her team in County Clare

🐐 UNPASTEURISED GOAT'S MILK, ANIMAL RENNET

Small changes can have big effects, at least in the world of cheese. Saint Tola Ash is smaller than its big sister and is lightly dusted with wood ash. Historically, adding the ash may have been a way to keep flies off, but it does seem to have an effect on the character of the cheese – the alkaline ash perhaps reducing the acidity of the paste, creating a more hospitable environment for the mould rind to develop. And what a rind this cheese has, promiscuously wrinkly from the predominance of the *Geotrichum*, with a coat of churchy grey mould overlaying the black of the ash, and glistening with moisture.

With all that going on, I was setting myself up for something quite hefty, but this cheese is confoundingly delicate, with a mild yoghurty acidity, a bare trace of goat and a green vegetable finish without the brassic edge I would expect from all that *Geo*. Being a smaller cheese, the action of the mould has penetrated more throughly into the paste, lowering the acidity and creating a more open texture. It is so fluffy it falls apart as you cut it, and it melts away in your mouth like the memory of clouds.

# Sinodun Hill

## Made by Rachel Yarrow and Fraser Norton in Oxfordshire

UNPASTEURISED GOAT'S MILK, VEGETARIAN RENNET

I tend to enjoy Sinodun Hill when it's still quite young, when there is little breakdown and the paste remains firm with fresh delicate flavours. The batch I tried for this book was more mature, as I could see from the sunken sides of its pyramidical form, and the dusting of blue overlaying the fawn colour of its tightly wrinkled *Geotrichum* rind. The paste smelled of Pista Burfi – the South Asian pistachio fudge – and this flavour was very present in the cheese, while the creamy breakdown added spice and peppery heat. The thick mousse texture is cut through with a fresh burst of acidity and a resinous note from the blueing provides an interesting finish.

That this older cheese retained balance and subtlety is a tribute to the cheesemakers' art. Rachel and Fraser use a natural rennet derived from the Cardoon thistle, used in Portuguese farmhouse cheesemaking and popularised in the British Isles by a Somerset cheesemaker, the late Mary Holbrook. I love that, after the near loss of artisan cheesemaking in the British Isles, a lineage is developing once more, in that Mary taught cheesemaker Caroline Atkinson, who in turn helped Rachel and Fraser to get started.

# The Cheese With No Name

## Made by Tom Humphris and Paul Bedford in Shropshire

 PASTEURISED COW'S MILK, VEGETARIAN RENNET

How can you name cheese? This is a frank response and a fine creation, completely enveloped in *Penicillium candidum* and seemingly without trace of any other pesky opportunistic microorganisms. It becomes clear why when you cut into the cheese. There is very little breakdown; this cheese is all soul, and the soul isn't dry, crumbly, unripened cheese but instead has the rich heavy texture of clotted cream – this is a *triple-crème*, with extra double cream added to the milk.

The flavour is wonderfully clean, and while the texture is opulently creamy it has a light acidic freshness. *Triple-crème* is a style that works best with none of the cabbage or edginess from *Geotrichum*, but it turns out that Tom does add *Geo*. In fact it's a 50/50 mix of that and the *P. camemberti*, and while this adds some complexity the cheeses are designed to be sold young while they are still pure white with a clean delicate flavour. Rarely for a cheese, I would suggest serving this slightly cool so that the texture retains its integrity and the clean fresh flavours are to the fore, as from a coolbox at a summer picnic with a nice glass of something crisp or sparkling.

# Tor

## Made by Roger Longman in Somerset

🐐 UNPASTEURISED GOAT'S MILK, ANIMAL RENNET

Named for Glastonbury Tor, this tall slim pyramid looks like a
Neolithic monument – the shape of a classic French Valencay.
A story goes that Valençay cheeses used to have pointy tops
like the pyramid of Giza, but these were sliced off in 1801 so
that Napoleon wouldn't be reminded of his defeat in Egypt.
Anyone who believes that has never tried to balance a pointy-
ended cheese mould on a draining table.

Like its French cousin, the goat is strong in this one, I get
the fulsome whiff of a goat barn on the rind and the creamy
well-broken-down paste has
more goat, pepper and enough
spicy heat in the long finish
to cause a slight catch in the
throat.

As an example of the
seeming magic of cheese-
making, the only difference
between this and Roger
Longman's Driftwood
goat's cheese logs is the
shape of the moulds.
The rest of the recipe is
identical, yet the cheeses emerge with quite different flavour
profiles – largely because of the different surface-to-mass ratio
in each cheese. Both are traditional shapes for French goat's
cheese styles and, as Roger says, 'they were that shape for a
reason'.

# Triple Rose

## Made by the Wright family in County Armagh

🐄 PASTEURISED COW'S MILK, VEGETARIAN RENNET

Triple Rose has a nice balance of snowy *Penicillium camemberti* and a trace of wrinkly *Geo.* on the rind. *Triple-crèmes* – of which this is one – rely more on texture than complexity of flavour for their sensory pleasure, and it is as well to keep flavours simple; the wrinkle of *Geo.* just adds a little depth. The added cream imparts a luxuriance to the texture of this indulgent cheese. What is less common in *triple-crèmes* is a bright lemony note that lifts the flavour and seems to clear the palate, making room for another bite.

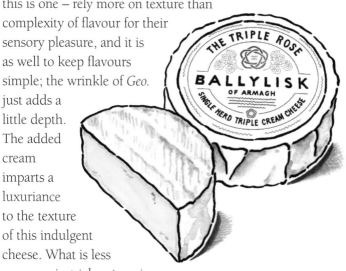

   The Wright family began farming in County Armagh in 1820 and Dean was the fifth generation, though the first to make cheese. He began studying cheesemaking in 2017, then in 2018 won three awards at the Irish Food Awards, which is about as steep a learning curve as it gets. Very sadly, in 2021, at the young age of 48, Dean passed away. His family have decided to carry on making Triple Rose and his last new cheese, Ballylisk Brie, so the legacy of this great cheesemaker will live on.

# Tunworth

## Made by Stacey Hedges and Charlotte Spruce in Hampshire

UNPASTEURISED COW'S MILK, ANIMAL RENNET

You only have to look at a Tunworth, with its attractively dappled wrinkly rind, to know you're in for a fulfilling experience. The paste has a rich mouth-filling texture and flavours of earth, cooked cabbage and, in older cheeses, caramelised onions and a spicy ammonia hit.

Stacey Hedges had been making curd cheese from the milk of her two goats when she saw a talk by eminent cheese teacher Val Bines. Val ended up coming over and they made cheese together in a saucepan in Stacey's kitchen, followed by a three day one-on-one teaching session, after Val had asked the question every aspiring cheesemaker needs to hear: 'Do you *really* want to make cheese?'

Stacey said yes and partnered with another aspiring cheesemaker, Julie Cheyney – who now has her own business making Saint Jude. They embarked on a market research programme which consisted of asking cheesemongers what was missing from the British cheeseboard and then visiting the Camembert makers of Normandy where they were inspired by their 'meticulous and beautiful' ladling skills. The milk comes from a herd of mixed Friesians and Swiss Browns who graze on old leys, seeded with a complex mix of grasses.

# Wicklow Bán

## Made by John and Bernie Hempenstall in County Wicklow

🐄 PASTEURISED COW'S MILK, VEGETARIAN RENNET

The gentle wrinkled rind with its white overlay tells me that *Geotrichum* and *Penicillium* are finely balanced in this cheese. The paste is pale for a cow's milk, and I wonder if this colour expresses the windswept salty pastures where the Hempenstall's sixty pedigree Friesians graze. Perfectly broken down, the cheese melts away in the mouth delightfully and, opening with a slight ammoniac tang, a flavour of hay develops, ending on a note of fresh bread. Even for such a delicate cheese, the flavour has length, persisting for a moment after you have finished the morsel – the sign of high quality cheese.

The Hempenstalls, dairy farmers for fifty years, began cheesemaking in 2005 as a response to the falling price of milk. They got their just deserts at the 2015 British Cheese Awards, when they won a gold medal for Wicklow Bán.

*Bán*, by the way, is Irish Gaelic for 'white', to distinguish this cheese from the Hempenstalls' other cheeses, Wicklow Blue and Wicklow Gold. Sometimes, you can't beat on-the-nose cheese naming.

# Wigmore

## Made by Anne and Andy Wigmore in Berkshire

UNPASTEURISED SHEEP'S MILK, VEGETARIAN RENNET

Wigmore is a washed-curd cheese. This means that some of the whey is run off and warm water added, resulting in a silky texture to the paste of the finished cheese. Removing the whey also results in lower acidity, giving a mellow sweetness to the flavour. Younger Wigmores have a pure white rind, showing the predominance of *Penicillium camemberti*, and have a mild flavour with a hint of button mushrooms from the rind, sweet milk and floral notes. Older ones begin to develop brown flecks on the rind, and have a deeper more complex flavour, suggesting the presence of other helpful moulds and yeasts. In a very mature Wigmore the paste liquifies and will start to ooze out of a cut piece, ultimately leaving you with nothing but a rind. You'd really want to eat a piece like that in one sitting, which is fine – it's a lovely cheese.

While many cheesemakers of the 1970s and 1980s Cheese Renaissance were urban refugees or farmers looking to add value to their milk, Anne Wigmore started out as a microbiologist and experimental cheesemaker at the National Institute for Research in Dairying, a rigorous foundation that might explain why she makes cheeses of such accomplished elegance.

# Winslade

## Made by Stacey Hedges and Charlotte Spruce in Hampshire

PASTEURISED COW'S MILK, ANIMAL RENNET

Like a Vacherin, Winslade has a binding of spruce bark. But Stacey and Charlotte don't wash their cheese. *B. linens* is therefore not dominant and a barely believable seventeen moulds, bacteria and yeasts play their part in creating Winslade's complex nuanced flavours.

The cheeses are plump and giving to the touch and the white mould has completely grown over the spruce band. The texture is indulgently creamy – like melting fondant icing – and the flavour is very clean, with a fresh uncooked cabbage note from the mould ripening and a slight meaty hint of *B. linens*. The piney flavour of the spruce bark is apparent from the start but sits in balance with the other flavours, coming through a bit more on the finish. Stacey and Charlotte soak the spruce so that the resinous flavour is softened, a traditional practice among French cheese-makers.

Vacherin is eminently seasonal, only available in the autumn and winter, and if you happen to be missing it in the summer you will be happy to know that Winslade is made all year round.

# Witheridge

## Made by Rose Grimond and her team in Oxfordshire

🐄 PASTEURISED COW'S MILK, ANIMAL RENNET

Witheridge, named for a small hamlet near Rose Grimond's farm, is aged in a singular way for a British cheese: it is matured in hay. As an example of the lengths to which cheesemakers will go, the hay comes from a single field sown with a particularly aromatic grass which is dried and toasted after harvesting. This gives a marvellous aroma to the rind – late summer meadow combining with the yeasty note of fresh straw on a barn floor, while the fermented toasty notes mingle with a hint of chocolate, producing an aroma of champagne truffles.

These flavours combine with the white pepper and a malty edge from the rind to build a spicy astringent finish, and would combine nicely with beer. Its makers describe Witheridge as a Cheddar style but I find its paste much softer, with a mouth-coating texture of ganache.

Maturing cheese in hay is actually an Italian habit and the mountain sheep's cheese Pecorino is sometimes finished in this way. As a cow's milk cheese, Witheridge is a novel hybrid – not so much Cheese Renaissance as Postmodern.

# Blue
# cheeses

# Blue cheeses

Barkham Blue . . . . . . . . . . . . .70

Bath Blue . . . . . . . . . . . . . . . .71

Beauvale Blue . . . . . . . . . . . . .72

Beenleigh Blue . . . . . . . . . . . .73

Binham Blue . . . . . . . . . . . . . .74

Blue Monk . . . . . . . . . . . . . . .75

Bluemin White . . . . . . . . . . . .76

Boyne Valley Blue . . . . . . . . . .77

Buffalo Blue . . . . . . . . . . . . . .78

Burt's Blue . . . . . . . . . . . . . . .79

Cashel Blue . . . . . . . . . . . . . .80

Colston Bassett Stilton . . . . . .81

Cote Hill Blue . . . . . . . . . . . . .82

Crozier Blue . . . . . . . . . . . . . .83

Darling Blue . . . . . . . . . . . . . .84

Dorset Blue Vinney . . . . . . . . .85

Hebridean Blue . . . . . . . . . . . .86

Lanark Blue . . . . . . . . . . . . . .87

Leeds Blue . . . . . . . . . . . . . . .88

Ludlow Blue . . . . . . . . . . . . . .89

Mon Las Anglesey Blue . . . . . .90

Mrs Bell's Blue . . . . . . . . . . . .91

Oxford Blue . . . . . . . . . . . . . .92

Remembered Hills . . . . . . . . . .93

Shropshire Blue . . . . . . . . . . . .94

Sparkenhoe Blue . . . . . . . . . . .95

Stichelton . . . . . . . . . . . . . . .96

Wicklow Blue . . . . . . . . . . . . .97

Young Buck . . . . . . . . . . . . . .98

# Blue cheeses

Once upon a time there was a shepherd guarding his flock. Lunchtime approached and he got his simple meal of bread and fresh cheese out of his sack only to see a gang of bandits coming over the hill towards him. Hiding his lunch under a rock, he ran off, leaving the sheep to their fate. Some days later the shepherd returned to get his lunch back and found that the bread had gone mouldy and some of the mould had got onto the cheese. Being hungry, he tried it and found it was good. He had discovered blue cheese. The lucky shepherd then spent some time experimenting with getting bread mould onto or into cheese before setting up a hugely successful blue cheese business, paying other people to look after his sheep.

This story is common to many cheesemaking cultures, although there are some national variations. For instance, in Italy there are no bandits and the shepherd nips off to visit his lover. (Also I added the bit about the blue cheese start-up). While this story does have a ring of the fairy tale about it, I think there are some elements of truth. I'm sure that, as for many families of cheeses, blues came about by accident rather than design. The mould in a blue cheese is the same one that you find on bread. It's called *Penicillium roqueforti* after the famous French blue cheese. Some traditional cheesemakers still get their blue spores from bread, but most modern cheesemakers use bought *Penicillium roqueforti* cultures for the sake of a predictable ripening path and consistency, which come in sachets of freeze-dried powder that are added to the milk in the vat. During maturation most cheeses are pierced with steel rods, thus allowing oxygen into the paste and encouraging mould growth. The piercing also ensures a thorough and even spread of blue veins throughout the cheese.

Blues can be roughly divided into four types. Least common are un-pierced *surface-ripened blues*, like the Bell family's Bluemin White, made in Yorkshire. Then there are the soft cheeses like Cote Hill Blue or the Irish Wicklow Blue, known generically as *blue bries*. These tend to have only one or two streaks of blue running horizontally through the paste, and the blue flavour is usually quite mild. Rindless *high-moisture* cheeses like the French Roquefort or the Devonian Beenleigh Blue are matured in a wrapping, often foil. In these cheeses the blue will tend to manifest in wider stripes and pockets in the paste. Finally there are the *rinded cheeses* like Stilton, which tend to be drier and firmer, in which the blue grows in long thin veins producing a marbled effect.

Generally, blue cheeses are relatively high in moisture; the curd is not heated and is cut into large cubes rather than the smaller grains needed for hard cheese. These techniques result in a more open texture that allows the blue to spread through the cheese. Blue cheeses tend to start out with quite a high acidity and a firm texture, and the ripening effect of the *Penicillium roqueforti*, together with other moulds and yeasts, both lowers acidity and makes the paste softer and more creamy.

Alongside these categories, blue cheese can be made from the milk of various animals, and the different characteristics of those milks will have an effect on flavour and texture. Most common in the British Isles are cow's milk blues, followed by sheep's and then goat's milk.

When buying blue cheeses, there are a few things to look out for. As with all cheeses, goat's milk will tend to be pure white, sheep's milk ivory, and cow's milk creamy yellow. The type of milk will have an effect on flavour; for example, if the goaty tang is not to your taste you will know to avoid very white cheese. Sheep's milk can often confer a piquant flavour, as can *Penicillium roqueforti*, leading to a whole lot of piquancy, particularly in older cheeses; for example, an aged Lanark Blue is well known for its sinus clearing properties.

The shade of the mould can also tell you a thing or two about flavour. Lighter blue, about the shade of a pair of stone-washed jeans, is milder with less piquancy and umami, and sometimes adds a bitter edge. Greenish veins are more intense and show more umami. The greenish tinge can also tell you that you are looking at a very freshly cut cheese. Without oxygen, the mould tends towards a greener tinge and turns blue when the cheese is cut and the face exposed to the air. Deep indigo mould will have the most intense flavour, with plenty of those piquant and umami notes.

More generally what I look for in the majority of blue cheeses is a fairly low proportion of blue to actual cheese, and a good even distribution of the blue veining. This is because what I am actually seeking is not the flavour of the blue mould itself but the flavour that results from the interaction of mould with cheese, and on the whole I want that flavour to be consistent throughout the cheese. Joe Schneider's Stichelton is a great example of this proportionate and even blueing; when cut, the paste looks like veined marble and the flavours are wonderfully complex yet not overpowering. However, all rules and guidelines about cheese are there to be broken or stretched. Hebridean Blue, for example, made on the Isle of Mull, is very heavily blued but is surprisingly restrained and complex for its appearance. Conversely, the blue-brie-style Wicklow Blue has only a single discreet line of blue rather than a thorough veining, yet the flavour pervades the whole cheese, and in the Irish Stilton-style Young Buck, the blue comes in clumps, such that the flavour changes depending where you are in the cheese, which is quite exciting.

The spread of blue is very much up to the cheesemaker – it is the result of when, and how many times, the cheese is pierced. Letting the cheese mature for some time before the first piercing allows the paste itself to develop complexity, and the fewer times the cheese is pierced during maturation, the less comprehensive the spread of blue will be. Joe Schneider waits for several weeks before piercing his Stichelton cheeses, and only pierces them twice during the three or four months of their maturation. They are wonderfully complex.

The important thing to remember about blue cheese is that it is *mould-ripened*. What distinguishes it from cheeses like Camembert and Brie is that the mould does its work from within, so blues are also known as *internally ripened* cheeses. This means that the most interesting flavours are not from the blue itself but arise from the interaction of the mould with the cheese. Broadly speaking the dominant notes in blue cheese are piquancy, largely down to ammonia, umami, from the breakdown of proteins into amino acids and fruitiness from the production of esters. This is why a really good Stilton like Colston Bassett can be spicy with notes of Marmite and bubblegum.

Of course, there can be many more flavours than those three in a Stilton or any other blue cheese. Contemporary microbiology teaches us that the ripening process involves the microbiota of a cheese – the entire collection of moulds, bacteria and yeasts – and how those microorganisms interact with each other rather than their individual flavours or actions. This is why a heavily blued cheese, where the *Penicillium roqueforti* has come out in front of any other microorganisms, might be one-dimensional. Ammonia is the ultimate breakdown product of the amino acids, and in a heavily blued and very mature cheese an eye-watering hit of ammonia can dominate all the other flavours. For anyone who has been been traumatised by a cheese like that, I suggest attempting a lightly blued more gentle cheese like Cashel Blue, which may lead one back into the fold.

As well as adding flavour, the mould lowers acidity and softens texture, so younger cheeses will tend to be more acidic and firmer. On the whole I prefer a cheese where the acidity has softened and the paste broken down into a more fondant-like texture. At the same time the acidity in a young cheese can add a pleasing freshness to the flavour profile.

One other contribution to complexity in blue cheese is that there are actually multiple strains of *Penicillium roqueforti*, which seem to behave differently in terms of how fast they grow and how vigorous their ripening action is. A 2017 study noted 210 strains which had been isolated from different cheeses. Historically, cheesemakers had a hand in fostering this diversity in that they took samples of moulds from their favourite cheeses and grew them on bread, such that each dairy would create and foster its own strain – a sort of unnatural selection.

# Barkham Blue

## Made by Sandy and Andy Rose in Berkshire

🐾 PASTEURISED COW'S MILK, ANIMAL RENNET

Barkham Blue's makers describe their cheese as 'ammonite shaped', though to me it looks appropriately like a piece of lichen-covered limestone. And it has a musty aroma reminiscent of an old bookshop – my spiritual home. The blue is a deep indigo and distributed in wide stripes and pockets throughout the creamy paste, itself a rich yellow from the Jersey and Guernsey milk the Roses use.

Flavours open with an appetising burst of salt and develop a verdant woody note; the rich fondant texture covers the palate and delivers a savoury tang of Marmite, while peppery heat builds to an exciting finish.

Unlike many modern British cheesemakers who came to the profession from seemingly random backgrounds, Sandy Rose actually grew up on a Berkshire dairy farm. Sensibly, she and Andy started out with a simple fresh goat's cheese made in a bucket in the kitchen and drained in muslin in the shower. This may sound very modern, but I suspect was not so distant from many an ancient practice.

# Bath Blue

## Made by Hugh Padfield and his team in Somerset

PASTEURISED COW'S MILK, ANIMAL RENNET

The paste of Bath Blue is ochre, with ivory patches around the blue which grows in knotted chains, such that the overall effect is like faded wallpaper. The aroma is of digestive biscuits and overall is rich and sweet with spicy notes from the dark indigo blue and an animal note leading to a hot, slightly ammoniated finish.

The cheeses are hand-pierced by Hugh Padfield's team, who refused the offer of a machine, saying that cleaning it would take as much time as the manual process. Apparently they enjoy this laborious task, which also gives them more control over the blueing. They can feel the texture of each cheese and if it's harder they make more holes to spread the blue more thoroughly.

The Padfields have been farming their land since 1914 and, after an eighty-year break, began cheesemaking again in the 1990s. Their signature cheese, Bath Soft, was inspired by a letter from Edmund Nelson to his better-known son Horatio in which he praises a cream cheese from Bath, which I like to imagine he ate in a dining room papered with the chinoiserie wallpaper fashionable at the time.

# Beauvale Blue

## Made by Robin Skailes and Howard Lucas in Nottinghamshire

🐾 PASTEURISED COW'S MILK, ANIMAL RENNET

This cheese is made at Cropwell Bishop Creamery, which is located in the beautiful Vale of Belvoir, ancient home of Stilton, and long famous for the production of that noble cheese.

Beauvale is softer, creamier and more delicately flavoured than Stilton, and has much in common with the Italian Gorgonzola Dolcelatte. The mould rind is soft and grey-blue with a lovely aroma of honey, and the paste, more broken down by that rind than a Stilton, has a wonderfully unctuous texture and fresh sour cream flavour. The softening action of the rind doesn't penetrate fully, leaving some firmer areas in the paste which add estery, banana and bright citrusy notes to the flavour profile. The blue is a light shade with less of the spicy and umami notes a darker blue would add, and people who aren't so keen on blues would have a great time with this cheese. The finish is long and the honey note of the rind returns for a final flourish.

For its mildness, I would try Beauvale early in a cheese-tasting session and it would make a fine ingredient in a creamy pasta sauce or a luxuriant topping for a burger.

# Beenleigh Blue

## Made by Ben Harris and Robin Congdon in Devon

PASTEURISED SHEEP'S MILK, VEGETARIAN RENNET

Fruity, floral and sweet with a texture like soft fudge ... you could be forgiven for thinking I was describing a dessert rather than a cheese. In fact, I reckon you could make an ice-cream with Beenleigh, which might be nice with a bit of Pedro Ximénez sherry drizzled over it. If someone does make this successfully, I will invite them round for dinner.

This sweetness, and the delicacy of the blue flavour, make Beenleigh a real gateway blue cheese, and will have you sampling the rustic delights of a cheese like the Spanish Cabrales in no time. But don't think that mildness signifies a lack of sophistication. This singular and complex cheese will hold its own on any cheeseboard. Robin Congdon, who began making the cheese in the 1970s, was one of the harbingers of the Cheese Renaissance and helped to revive the long-defunct practice of milking sheep in Britain. He is also the originator of a quote that to me perfectly expresses the Zen of cheesemaking: 'The cheesemaker only guides the milk in the direction it wants to go.'

# Binham Blue

## Made by Catherine Temple in Norfolk

🐾 PASTEURISED COW'S MILK, VEGETARIAN RENNET

Binham has a grey velvet-textured rind with a slightly animal smell rather than the musty parish church aroma I'd expect from a mould-ripened cheese of that colour. Its paste is a creamy yellow from the rich Swiss Brown milk, which is combined in this cheese with the milk from their Friesian-Holsteins. The blue presents in pockets and stripes rather than the veins you'd see in a Stilton style and the flavour is complex yet delicate with sweet notes of malted milk and caramel.

Catherine Temple began as a pharmacist and, when you consider the science that good cheesemaking requires, the move makes sense. In fact, she still manages to juggle both careers, showing a command of multi-tasking that explains how she makes eight different and equally excellent cheeses on the farm. Traditional cheesemaking has always had a frugal elegance about it – the whey was fed to pigs, whose dung fed the land. In the same spirit, the Temples use an anaerobic digester to convert waste products from livestock and cheesemaking into heat and power, and fine natural fertiliser for their fields.

# Blue Monk

## Made by Karen and Mark Hindle in Herefordshire

🐾 UNPASTEURISED COW'S MILK, ANIMAL RENNET

Blue Monk is named for a tune by my favourite pianist, Thelonious Monk, so it's a winner with me from the start. Just looking at its rind, with its brainy-wrinkled texture overlaying a dark blue and verdigris coloured surface, makes me think of his gnarly yet beautiful compositions. Expecting a mighty aroma, I was struck by its delicacy – musty, with a slight tang of ammonia and a blue note. The paste is ivory white – pale for a cow's milk – and is well broken down, with the blue spreading in straight lines from the piercings and gathering in small pockets. The aroma of the paste makes me think of bath salts – a combination of floral and mineral notes – and that minerality continues in the flavour along with a bracing tart acidity.

We have chance and a few drinks to thank for the existence of these cheeses. In 1988, after a night of 'generous hospitality', Karen and Mark decided to buy a cheese shop in Leominster called Mousetrap. Discovering a dearth of locally made cheese, they decided to make their own and, after a few lessons from a retired cheese teacher, Karen began making cheese in their kitchen. They set up their dairy, Monkland Cheese, in 1996.

# Bluemin White

## Made by the Bell family in Yorkshire

🐄 PASTEURISED COW'S MILK, VEGETARIAN RENNET

Bluemin White is un-pierced – a rare example of a British surface-ripened blue, and an idea Katie Bell came up with. It is one of the most striking cheeses I've ever seen, with its thick coat of olive grey mould overlaying a tight wrinkle of *Geotrichum* and a sunburst pattern forming in the mould on the top. Against the a dark rind the rich yellow of the paste makes a startling contrast. The breakdown is thorough, but for such a ripe-looking cheese the aroma is gentle with just a hint of mustiness from the rind. In the mouth the texture is buttery and mouth-filling, with a hot sensation up front giving way to sweetness and a rich grassy flavour.

The star-shaped pattern is an unintended consequence – the imprint of the cheese mould. An acceptance of the accidental, happy or not, is a necessary part of cheesemaking and fosters a certain humility in all the best cheesemakers. As Katie's sister Caroline says, 'Cheesemaking and maturing humbles you. It doesn't matter if you think you're on top of it, nature will always throw you a curveball.' It looks like they caught this one.

# Boyne Valley Blue

## Made by Michael Finnegan in County Louth

 PASTEURISED GOAT'S MILK, VEGETARIAN RENNET

Boyne Valley Blue has an excitingly multicoloured rind, slightly furred with patches of blue, and the overall effect is of pinkish grey parchment. The paste is a pale ivory, the blueing is light, growing mainly down the few straight tracks of the piercing rods. The aroma is predominantly of honey with a little must and ammonia from the rind. In the mouth, the texture is moist, slightly crumbly, with a light bounce, which suggests careful gentle treatment of the curd.

The flavour is delicate for a blue goat's cheese, opening with a clean sweetness, swiftly developing old country church, a light trace of goat to keep things interesting, and finishing on a biscuity flavour like wheat crackers. The salting is excellent, quite noticeable all the way through, though never too much and helping to bring out all the flavours.

Michael Finnegan sent his milk to another dairy before taking over the cheesemaking himself in 2016. Originally he made his Boyne Valley only in the summer and his older cheeses tended to get a bit pokey. But by staggering the kidding in his herd Michael can make this cheese all year round now and sell it at around one or two months, when it is mild enough to appeal to all.

# Buffalo Blue

## Made by the Bell family in Yorkshire

⚘ PASTEURISED WATER BUFFALO MILK, VEGETARIAN RENNET

I imagine water buffalo to be possessed of a massive dignity and, while slow to anger, capable of great fierceness. At least that's what I got from the character of the cheese. The rind shows a dark heavy coat of blue mould and the paste is snow white, showing the rich creaminess of buffalo milk in its luxuriant texture. In the mouth the texture is like clotted cream, with a startling crunch from the veins and pockets of blue and a sweet malty flavour like digestive biscuits. Buffalo Blue also has a unique sense of timing. Instead of slowly building in intensity, everything continues mildly and then ends in a sudden burst of spicy pepper.

You don't see many water buffalo around in the British Isles, nor their cheeses for that matter. They aren't native to Europe and may have arrived on the continent as a gift from the khan of the Avars to an Italian king in the year 600 CE. The rarity of their cheese might be because the range you can make from high fat milk is limited – the most famous one would be the Italian Mozzarella di Bufala.

# Burt's Blue

## Made by Claire Burt in Cheshire

 PASTEURISED COW'S MILK, VEGETARIAN RENNET

I like the smaller version of this cheese – the Baby Burt's Blue – which comes in a plump disc, like a tempting little pie. The rind has a brainy wrinkle and is mostly blue-grey with very little white, showing the dominance of *Penicillium roqueforti* and *Geotrichum*. The aroma on the rind is predominantly blue with a comforting hint of old books.

Burt's Blues are hand-pierced and the blue grows in two neat horizontal lines throughout the paste. The paste is interestingly pale for a cow's milk with plenty of creamy breakdown, though a trace of the firm centre still persists and adds a lightness to the flavour. The blue flavour is very gentle, with more of the mushroomy scent of a forest floor than any spicy overtones, also imparting a malty biscuit note, and overall the flavour is sweet and milky with a slight refreshing bitterness running through it. Perhaps pies are in my mind because of the shape, but I really fancy wrapping the whole cheese in pastry and baking it in the oven.

# Cashel Blue

**Made by Geurt van den Dikkenberg and the Grubb Family in County Tipperary**

🏵 PASTEURISED COW'S MILK, VEGETARIAN RENNET

Rich, buttery, with a restrained blueing, Cashel is a very moreish cheese. The gentle blue flavour makes it another great starter cheese for anyone beginning their blue odyssey or a fresh beginning for someone whose taste buds have been thrown by a particularly fierce example. It's perhaps not surprising that this is such a lush cheese given Ireland's luxuriant pasture – it's no wonder they call it the Emerald Isle.

Cheesemakers and farmers are an enterprising lot. Faced with the Sisyphean task of turning hundreds of cheeses every day, Louis Grubb invented a mechanism for turning whole shelves at a time. Along with the Giant's Causeway, Newgrange and James Joyce's Martello Tower, a visit to the cheese-turning machine is a must-see destination for any cheesemonger visiting Ireland. On the subject of visits, in 2012 Queen Elizabeth II made a state visit to Ireland on the invitation of the President, the first for a hundred years. At the ceremonial banquet the chef served Cashel Blue, which made quite the impression on the Queen. She name-checked it on a trip to Cork Market, where she called Prince Philip over to look at all the lovely Irish cheeses.

# Colston Bassett Stilton

## Made by Billy Kevan and his team in Nottinghamshire

PASTEURISED COW'S MILK, ANIMAL OR VEGETARIAN RENNET

The thing that you need to know about Stilton is that when Scott went on his first voyage to the Antarctic he took twelve whole Stiltons with him, and he came back. On his second voyage, he didn't take any, and he didn't come back. The moral of this story is pretty clear.

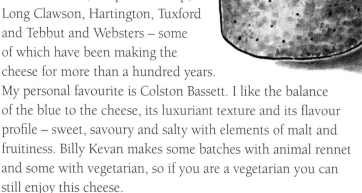

There are six Stilton producers – Colston Bassett, Cropwell Bishop, Long Clawson, Hartington, Tuxford and Tebbut and Websters – some of which have been making the cheese for more than a hundred years. My personal favourite is Colston Bassett. I like the balance of the blue to the cheese, its luxuriant texture and its flavour profile – sweet, savoury and salty with elements of malt and fruitiness. Billy Kevan makes some batches with animal rennet and some with vegetarian, so if you are a vegetarian you can still enjoy this cheese.

Other Stiltons can be firmer, show more acidity or, if you prefer a more intense piquancy, more blueing. Their rumpled knobbly coat can range in colour from grey, through fawn to an exciting shade of pink that some of us mongers like to call baboon's bum (but maybe don't try this phrase out on your local cheese shop, unless you're on first name terms).

# Cote Hill Blue

## Made by the Davenport family in Lincolnshire

UNPASTEURISED COW'S MILK, VEGETARIAN RENNET

Market research is indispensable. In the Davenport family's case this consisted of bumping into a Waitrose buyer on a cheesemaking course who told them that what Britain needed was more soft blues. Luckily for the Davenports they didn't know that this is a notoriously difficult style to make, and their very first attempt at cheesemaking turned out so well that they stuck to the recipe ever since. 'It was only when someone at a Specialist Cheesemakers Association meeting asked how many batches we'd had to make before we got a good one that I realised how lucky we were,' Mary told me.

I'd actually place this cheese in the blue brie category. Its velvety gunmetal grey rind with a pronounced wrinkle of *Geotrichum* might confound those who expect a brie to be white, but this is how the old-style farmhouse bries used to look. The paste has the rich yellow of Wall's vanilla ice-cream, and a single line of blue runs horizontally through the cheese, the result of a single piercing done by hand. This is an intense cheese: its thick cream texture delivers a cowy whiff, a peppery hit from the blue and an enlivening edge of minerality.

# Crozier Blue

## Made by Geurt van den Dikkenberg and the Grubb family in County Tipperary

 PASTEURISED COW'S MILK, VEGETARIAN RENNET

As a monger, I am more cheese fancier than businessman, and my liking for the crazier creations of cheesemakers is perhaps a manifestation of this divide. When I was a younger monger, back in the early-noughties, Crozier Blue was bonkers – heavily blued, dripping with peppery juice, and with an intensity that began by burning your mouth and finished by leaving it numb. I loved it, but poor old Crozier never sold as well as its more delicate sibling Cashel, and in recent years it has become much more restrained.

Going by looks, you might still think you're in for a wild ride. The cheese is very moist with a thorough blueing, but the gentle aroma of digestive biscuits belies the rambunctious appearance. Crozier is sweet, but not floral, the malty biscuit flavour persists, finishing with a spicy hit of blue, a trace of sheepiness, and just a whisper of ammonia. However, as if to reassure me that Crozier retains a memory of its swashbuckling past, even after the last flavour has faded, I am left with a singular sensation – the tip of my tongue is tingling and numb as if I had bitten into a Szechuan peppercorn.

# Darling Blue

## Made by Maggie Maxwell in Northumberland

🦋 PASTEURISED COW'S MILK, ANIMAL RENNET

Maggie Maxwell's cheese-naming is impressive. This one is a nod to the nineteenth-century heroine Grace Darling, a lighthouse-keeper's daughter who saved the survivors of a ship wrecked off the Northumbrian coast.

Although the cheese looks quite fierce, it is really very friendly. Its rind, pitted, gnarly and rustically beautiful, has an aroma of biscuits, old bookshops and only a faint whiff of ammonia, and the blue grows in broad strips and tiny caves here and there throughout the paste. The blue flavour is very delicate with a slightly peppery flavour, and overall the cheese has a sweet malty flavour like a rich tea biscuit. As with Maggie's Cuddy's Cave, acidity and astringency build to an optimal level, and then rest there rather than increasing – and I am beginning to think that she has supernatural cheesemaking powers. However skilful you are, you need really good milk, and she recently bought a new bull called Derek, who is a Montbéliarde, a breed famed for their rich milk. 'He's quite a character,' Maggie told me, after deciding to change his name to Monty, which she thought more befitting to his dignity. In my mind, though, he will always be Derek the Bull.

# Dorset Blue Vinney

## Made by the Davies family in Dorset

PASTEURISED COW'S MILK, VEGETARIAN RENNET

Its very name – Dorset Vinney – locates this cheese in the ancient past of British cheesemaking. *Vinney* is a corruption of *vinew*, meaning 'mould', derived from a Middle English word and still in use in the sixteenth century. Historically, Dorset was more famed for its cream than its cheese, and in the old days Blue Vinney was a side-product; farmers would skim the cream off the milk and use the remainder for cheesemaking. Thorough blueing was commonly ensured by dragging a bit of mouldy horse harness through the vat – a hit-or-miss way of making cheese in which, as one farmer recalled, 'only ten out of fifty cheeses came off and the rest were as hard as bloody bullets'.

The replacement of hand-skimming by a mechanical process that left even less fat in the milk seems to have caused Blue Vinney's demise and by the 1970s it had disappeared. Happily, Michael Davies decided to revive this cheese, and sensibly hand-skims the milk for it. With a rough, fawn-orange rind and a deep well-distributed indigo blue, the cheese has an aroma of digestive biscuits, a satisfyingly chewy texture and a long hot peppery finish. I'm sure Michael's hit rate is better than one in five, too.

# Hebridean Blue

## Made by the Reade family on the Isle of Mull

UNPASTEURISED COW'S MILK, ANIMAL RENNET

When I unwrapped my first Hebridean Blue, I actually let out a barbaric yawp of delight at its thrillingly rustic, craggy appearance. As much as this is billed as a Scottish Stilton style, its paste is ivory rather than yellow and the blue is tightly packed, running throughout the cheese in thread veins rather than the fissures and caverns of blue mould in a Stilton. It is also a really dark colour – close to indigo – which reminds me of Cabrales, a rustic, mouth-burning cheese matured in caves in the mountains of northern Spain.

But the Hebridean Blue is very much its own creature. Its aroma is quite restrained, offering a muted maltiness, like an empty biscuit barrel, and the hot and spicy flavours level out, leaving just a slight tingling on the tongue at the finish. However, this is not a mild cheese! The comprehensive blueing brings an intensity to its flavour which includes a hefty ammoniac whiff felt in the back of the nose. Personally, I love this, and I would eat a ton of it, given the chance. But, if you are unsure of your gathering's appetite for blue cheese, I would leave this one for a bit. It is not one for the faint-hearted.

# Lanark Blue

## Made by Angela Cairns and the Erringtons in Lanarkshire

🐑 UNPASTEURISED SHEEP'S MILK, ANIMAL RENNET

A couple of centuries ago, Scotland used to be known for the production of a blue sheep's milk cheese that Walter Scott rated 'as good as Stilton'. This original Lanarkshire cheese was strong fare, by all acounts, and I wonder if Scott's patriotism overcame his judgement. Or maybe people had more robust palates in those days.

In the early 1980s, when Humphrey Errington left a cushy job in shipping law for the windswept, chilly and generally unremunerative lifestyle of a sheep-farming cheesemaker, he decided to revive Lanark Blue. All memory of the cheese was lost, so Humphrey went to study with the cheesemakers of Aveyron in southern France, producers of the world-famous Roquefort. This might seem like poor brand protection on the part of the French, but cheesemakers tend to be unusually generous of spirit. They also know that it is all but impossible to make an exact copy of a cheese, no matter how closely you follow the recipe. So Lanark has its own inimitable character, firmer and crunchier than Roquefort, and with a sharp acidity that can make it even more intense than its fierce French cousin.

# Leeds Blue

## Made by Mario Olianas in North Yorkshire

🐑 PASTEURISED SHEEP'S MILK, ANIMAL RENNET

The rumpled white rind of Leeds Blue looks rather like a stack of cumulonimbus clouds, with a dusting of greys and pinks on the top. Its paste is pale ivory and has a creamy lustre, with light blue-grey mould spread evenly in pockets rather than veins. All in all, there's an exuberantly Italian air about it, a cheese shouldering its way boisterously onto a British cheeseboard to the dismay of the more reserved natives.

Actually, the gentle malty aroma heralds a far less fierce cheese than its appearance suggests. The texture is a fascinating mix of the unctuous and elastic, and the blue surprisingly delicate, with a note of dried rosemary, a mineral edge and soft burst of peppery heat in the finish. If I sound surprised by Leeds Blue's delicacy, it's because as a blue sheep's milk I expected this cheese to have more in common with piquant and hot cheeses like Roquefort or Lanark Blue. That more of the volatile fatty acids responsible for those intense flavours have not been released is a tribute to the patience and gentleness of Mario's craft.

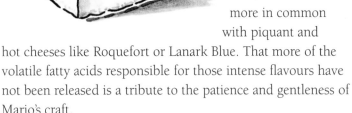

# Ludlow Blue

## Made by Tom Humphris and Paul Bedford in Shropshire

PASTEURISED COW'S MILK, VEGETARIAN RENNET, CARROT JUICE

The indigo mould runs in knotted chains and caves through the orange paste of Ludlow Blue, whose rough-textured, dark blue and verdigris-coloured rind reminds me of rocks in a tree-shaded river. The aroma is unthreatening, with a mere trace of ammonia and lots of rich tea biscuits. Sweetness comes first, followed by ammonia, and the firm texture breaks down creamily in the mouth, balancing the vigorous spicy heat. A savoury blue note and chocolatey warmth come next, with an astringent tingle in the finish.

Unlike any other cheese, the orange colour comes from carrot juice rather than annatto because Tom and Paul prefer to use local ingredients, and annatto is produced in South America. Another thing that marks this cheese out is the rubbing up, a process for rinded blue cheeses in which, when they are still very young, the outside is smoothed over with a knife to prevent cracking as the cheese matures. Ludlow Blue has very little rubbing up and does develop some cracks, so that the cheeses mature more quickly and don't really need to be pierced (though Tom and Paul pierce most cheeses for consistency's sake). Un-pierced blues are rare in Britain, or anywhere else for that matter, and it would be fascinating to try one.

# Mon Las Anglesey Blue

## Made by Menai Jones on Anglesey

🐄 PASTEURISED COW'S MILK, ANIMAL RENNET

Mon Las is inspired by Gorgonzola Dolcelatte but, as with all transplanted cheese styles, it has its own particular character – and indeed quite a lot more of it than its mild Italian model. A pronounced cowy aroma is perceptible from some distance, and the texture is thicker and more mouth-coating than Gorgonzola. The blue 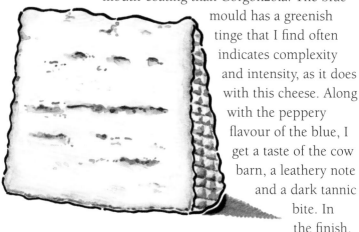 mould has a greenish tinge that I find often indicates complexity and intensity, as it does with this cheese. Along with the peppery flavour of the blue, I get a taste of the cow barn, a leathery note and a dark tannic bite. In the finish, sweetness comes through, and a slight bitterness, perhaps from the vegetarian rennet, that nicely ties the whole thing together.

When Menai Jones isn't making brilliant cheese, she runs the History department at the local Anglesey secondary school. Perhaps department heads have an affinity for cheesemaking, as her colleague Huw Davies, head of Maths, also makes cheese on the island.

# Mrs Bell's Blue

## Made by the Bell family in Yorkshire

UNPASTEURISED SHEEP'S MILK, ANIMAL RENNET

Celebrated by the admirably un-nationalistic French chef Raymond Blanc, Mrs Bell's is Yorkshire's answer to Roquefort. The paste is a pale ivory colour and the blue, in indigo and greenish shades, is distributed in wide streaks and pockets. On the nose there is a hint of biscuits and dried wildflowers, and the flavour, opening with an estery fruitiness, is sweet with notes of pepper and lanolin and a gentle ammoniac sensation throughout. Given the florid blueing, I was expecting to get much more of that ammonia in the nose, and the restrained flavour was another surprising thing about this singular cheese.

Judy Bell began making cheese on the family farm more than thirty years ago out of an interest in the nutritional benefits of sheep's milk – which can be easier to digest than cows. She bought six milking sheep and got some mentoring from a local cheesemaker, who was excited to explore sheep's cheesemaking, knowing of its ancient history in the region. That world-famous child of the Yorkshire Dales, Wensleydale, was originally a sheep's milk cheese, but by the 1980s sheep's cheeses were all but extinct in Britain. Mrs Bell's Blue was one of the harbingers of their revival.

# Oxford Blue

### Made by Butlers Farmhouse Cheese in Lancashire and matured by Baron Roger Pouget in Oxfordshire

🐄 PASTEURISED COW'S MILK, VEGETARIAN RENNET

Wrapped in a vine leaf, itself more British Racing Green than its Oxford Blue packaging, this high moisture cheese has small pockets of blue in a pale yellow paste. The blue flavour is very gentle, and is perfectly intertwined with notes of sweetness and malted milk. A trace of bitterness provides a pleasing contrast to the sweet note and lifts the rich creamy texture off the palate.

Baron Pouget, who in his past life was a film agent, decided to open a cheese shop in Oxford in 1984. In 1994 he decided to service a gap in the market by producing a soft creamy blue in the style of the soft French blue Saint Agur. A previous attempt at a soft blue by the Milk Marketing Board had resulted in the much maligned Lymeswold – brutally parodied by *Private Eye* as Slymeswold – whose widely celebrated demise in 1992 made room for this vastly more accomplished cheese, which won a gold at the British Cheese Awards in 1995. Oxford Blue highlights the role of the *affineur* in the production of cheese. It is made to Pouget's specification by Butlers and then travels down to the maturing rooms in Oxford, where it is given a final polish.

# Remembered Hills

## Made by Tom Humphris and Paul Bedford in Shropshire

PASTEURISED COW'S MILK, VEGETARIAN RENNET

The paste of Remembered Hills is a pale yellow and the blue spreads through the cheese in tight chains. The texture is firm and chewy with a sharp acidity and pepper up front, those sensations softening as the cheese breaks down in the mouth, developing flavours of winter barns and meatiness with a trace of sweet milk and caramel, and finishing on an astringent tingle.

The name comes from an A. E. Housman poem, 'Blue Remembered Hills', whose wistful tone puts me in mind of how the long finish of this cheese leaves a lingering memory. This was the cheese from which Tom and his old boss Dudley Lewis developed their Ludlow Blue, in response to a constant demand for the orange-coloured Shropshire Blue. The make  is essentially the same, but for the lack of carrot juice in this cheese, and a more thorough rubbing up, which creates a durable rind with less cracking. Attempting to assign effects to particular causes is a fool's errand when it comes to cheese, but I would say that the higher acidity in Remembered Hills might have something to do with that protective rind and how it allows the cheese to mature more slowly.

# Shropshire Blue

## Made by Billy Kevan and his team in Nottinghamshire

🐄 PASTEURISED COW'S MILK, VEGETARIAN RENNET

The orange colour from the annatto is given a muted duskiness by the blueing in this striking cheese, which runs through the paste in tight knotted chains. The intense indigo blue provides the predominant aroma, with a trace of mustiness from the rind. The texture is firm and chewy but melts in the mouth, delivering sweet milk, musty cellary notes, and a light burst of ammonia in the finish.

The origins of Shropshire Blue are somewhat curious. According to Scottish cheesemaker Humphrey Errington, it was inspired by Bleu d'Auvergne and invented by Janet Galloway, a teacher at the West of Scotland Agricultural College. It was originally made at Castle Stewart Dairy and known as Blue Stewart, but according to Humphrey it never took off and eventually the recipe was sold to Stilton makers Long Clawson, who, despite being based in Leicestershire, decided to call it Shropshire Blue. They still make this cheese, as do Cropwell Bishop Creamery, another venerable Stilton producer. Recently a family-run farm and dairy, the Shropshire Cheese Company, have been producing a version as well. According to my French informants the cheese is popular in France, so much so that some *fromagers* have chosen it to represent British cheese over Cheddar.

# Sparkenhoe Blue

## Made by Will Clarke in Warwickshire

 UNPASTEURISED COW'S MILK, ANIMAL RENNET

The pale paste of Sparkenhoe Blue shows a restrained blueing, the mould growing in narrow veins in the marbled effect typical of a classic Stilton style, though this one, being unpasteurised, cannot take that famous name. The aroma is forward, with notes of Marmite, tutti-frutti ice-cream and spritzy yoghurt. The chewy fondant texture delivers an impressively complex palate of flavours, beginning with coffee chocolate gateau, Marmite, citrus, and finishing with the aromatic burst of spice you get when roasting cumin seeds.

Will Clarke's parents began cheesemaking in 2005 with the revival of traditional farmhouse Red Leicester. Will's decision to develop a blue cheese in 2017 makes him the second generation of cheesemakers on their farm – an impressively short gap. Originally setting out to make an actual Stilton, the family bought a pasteuriser, which now sits unemployed in a corner of the dairy. The first batches, made with unpasteurised milk, were so good that Will decided to forgo the benefits of taking the Stilton name. His cheese shows all the depth and complexity you would expect from a skilfully made raw milk cheese.

# Stichelton

## Made by Joe Schneider and his team in Nottinghamshire

 UNPASTEURISED COW'S MILK, ANIMAL RENNET

Sweet like Hubba Bubba bubblegum, malty like Shreddies, savoury like Marmite, this fantastic cheese has the luxurious mouthfeel of fondant icing. The milk has a short commute from milking parlour to vat, arriving unruffled due to the slowness of the pump, and the curd is ladled by hand – a skilful and demanding job for Joe and his team. We can thank their patience, skill and fortitude for the rich creamy texture, while the complexity and depth of flavour is largely down to the health and happiness of the cows and that their top-quality milk is left in its natural unpasteurised state.

Everything about this cheese would qualify it to take the revered name of Stilton, as it's made to a traditional recipe in Nottinghamshire, one of the cheese's home counties.

Everything except the fact that it is made from raw milk. Since 1992, the Stilton Cheesemakers' Association has said that all Stilton must be pasteurised. Joe values the benefits, and accepts the vicissitudes of raw milk cheesemaking – the heights of complexity and deliciousness that can be achieved – over the status conferred by the hallowed brand, and calls his cheese after the old Anglo-saxon name for the town of Stilton, Stichelton.

# Wicklow Blue

## Made by John and Bernie Hempenstall in County Wicklow

PASTEURISED COW'S MILK, VEGETARIAN RENNET

Wicklow Blue is an example of the thorny issue of cheese classification. As a brie style with blue mould, is it a mould-ripened cheese or a blue? Its makers have helped us with the name, so into the blues it goes. The rind is pure white with no perceptible evidence of *Geotrichum*. If this is deliberate, I think it is a wise move, as there is plenty going on already with the blue, the *Penicillium* and the flavours in the paste.

The blueing in this cheese is admirably restrained, forming a couple of horizontal veins through the centre of the paste, and like their Wicklow Bán the texture is perfectly uniform, with no distinction between breakdown and paste. I get a gentle aroma of button mushrooms on the nose, and a clean milky flavour, with a further hint of those mushrooms.

The blue flavour has none of the savoury or piquant flavours you may be used to in more intense cheese like Stilton or Roquefort – you just get a comforting mustiness, as of the smell of an old book. In fact, everything about this cheese speaks of restraint and delicacy.

# Young Buck

## Made by Michael Thomson in County Down

UNPASTEURISED COW'S MILK, ANIMAL RENNET

Mike Thomson is a living warning of the unintended consequences of working in a deli – Arcadia in Belfast, where dreams of professional football and social work melted away in the presence of all that fine cheese. Once he'd found his true calling, Mike enrolled on the cheesemaking course at the Welbeck School of Artisan Food and made some great British cheeses, like Sparkenhoe Red Leicester, Tunworth and, fatefully, Joe Schneider's Stichelton.

Northern Ireland's artisan cheese industry was missing a raw milk blue and, having paid his dues, in 2013 Mike made his first cheese, a raw milk Stilton style named, somewhat cheekily, Young Buck. This has a powdery white rind, giving a slight ammoniac tang, joined with a malty sweet scent. The blue is well balanced with the paste, if a little unevenly distributed – Mike pierces his cheese by hand, with a kebab skewer rather than a machine. Mike, as I do, celebrates this rustic inconsistency. Different parts of the cheese have quite different flavours, from the white chocolate and estery banana notes of the paste, the spicy Marmite of the blue and the malty biscuit flavour near the rind.

# Washed-rind cheeses

# Washed-rind cheeses

Admiral Collingwood . . . . . .105
Baronet . . . . . . . . . . . . . . . .106
Drewi Sant. . . . . . . . . . . . . .107
Durrus. . . . . . . . . . . . . . . . .108
Edmund Tew . . . . . . . . . . . .109
Eve. . . . . . . . . . . . . . . . . . . .110
Gubbeen . . . . . . . . . . . . . . .111
Highmoor . . . . . . . . . . . . . .112
Lindum . . . . . . . . . . . . . . . .113
Little Rollright. . . . . . . . . . .114
Maida Vale. . . . . . . . . . . . . .115

Merry Wyfe of Bath . . . . . . . .116
Milleens. . . . . . . . . . . . . . . .117
Ogleshield . . . . . . . . . . . . . .118
Oxford Isis. . . . . . . . . . . . . .119
Rachel . . . . . . . . . . . . . . . . .120
Renegade Monk. . . . . . . . . .121
Saint Cera . . . . . . . . . . . . . .122
Saint James . . . . . . . . . . . . .123
Saval . . . . . . . . . . . . . . . . . .124
Stinking Bishop. . . . . . . . . .125
Westray Wife. . . . . . . . . . . .126

# Washed-rind cheeses

The washed-rinds are a divisive family of cheeses. For some, their pungent barnyardy whiff is the harbinger of deliciousness; others wonder how one could consider them to be a foodstuff. Actually the aroma of these often maligned cheeses is usually more intense than their actual flavour and, when you have tried a few, you may find that their scent becomes enticing rather than off-putting. And within the family there is considerable variation, from the near-liquid Stinking Bishop to the firm yet springy textured Gubbeen.

Washed-rind cheeses get more of their character from their maturing – the *affinage* – than from the cheesemaking, and their transformation from firm white cheeses with little flavour into creamy pink pungent little beasts is little short of magical. The *affinage* begins when the cheeses are firm and white and have had no time to develop a rind. The *affineur* dips a cloth into a bowl of brine, gives the top and sides of each cheese a gentle rub, and then flips it over to do the bottom. The salty water kills any mould spores that might be planning to create a mould-ripened

(Camembert-style) cheese, and creates an inviting environment for a bacterium called *Brevibacterium linens*, or *B. linens*, which is largely responsible for the orange-pink colour, sticky surface and the intense aromas and flavours that characterise this family. Modern *affineurs* often use bought strains of *B. linens*, as this ensures a more predictable path of ripening, and you can buy not only specific strains, but a tailor-made collection of bacteria, moulds and yeasts that give particular outcomes. Strains of *B. linens* are advertised as producing not just particular colours but also individual cheese types like Normandy or Alpine washed-rind styles. It's not necessary to use bought cultures, though. *B. linens* is so ubiquitous that merely washing the young cheeses can be enough to get the rind going.

Once you have some shelves of washed-rinds in your store, you can hurry the process along and create more consistency by giving older cheeses a rub with your wet salty cloth before moving on to the new ones, thus transferring the bacteria onto the new ones. Effectively, with this approach, you are selecting and propagating a particular strain of *B. linens* unique to your maturing room, giving your cheeses their own distinctive character. Yeasts and moulds add flavour and also have more complex and profound effects. *Geotrichum*, for example, not only makes its sulphuric cabbagey contribution but helps to lower acidity on the surface, a boon to *B. linens*, which flourishes in low acid conditions.

Cheeses are also often washed in booze, which traditionally would be produced in the same area as the cheese – the pudgy and wrinkled Langres is washed in Marc de Champagne, and Stinking Bishop in a perry made from a local variety of pear. Unsurprisingly for a cheese with monastic associations, beer is popular. Its relatively low alcohol doesn't interfere too much with microbial activity, and any yeasts and residual sugars in the beer might do their bit to help the ripening process. All the cheeses must always start off with some brine washing, however, so that a good microbial population is well established.

Washed-rind cheeses have a long association with monasticism, and their first flowering is thought to have been in the early medieval monasteries of northern France. This makes sense for a couple of reasons. You need a low acid cheese for the *B. linens* to grow, so that means working with fresh milk. Peasants didn't have many animals and so tended to keep the milk from more than one milking, making the resultant cheeses too acidic for the *B. linens* to take hold. Monasteries, on the other hand, had large flocks and herds and could begin making cheese straight after milking. Added to this, the process of washing is time-consuming and demands attention. With a team of lay workers to do the animal husbandry and milking, the brothers could focus on the cheesemaking and *affinage*. The dietary restrictions imposed by the orders may also have played a part. Monks had a pretty bland diet and you can imagine a proto-*affineur* monk developing a taste for pungent and meaty cheeses, for those days when meat and fish were forbidden.

It's probable that washed-rinds were made in dozens of British and Irish monasteries, as well as France, though due to their dissolution by Henry VIII in 1536 these cheese traditions were lost to time. After the Dissolution, monastic cheesemakers likely took their skills with them to secular businesses, but these, at the time, favoured larger and harder cheeses that could be transported to markets.

The reappearance of native washed-rind cheese in the British Isles is linked to the very first tentative steps in what became the Cheese Renaissance of the 1970s and 1980s. One of the first was the sticky, earthy and animalistic Milleens, made by doyenne of that movement Veronica Steele on her family's farm on the wet and salty coast of County Cork. Apparently, Veronica had been trying to make hard cheeses but they kept turning out soft, pink and smelly, so, giving into the demands of her *terroir*, Milleens was born. There was in fact a flowering of washed-rind cheese in County Cork at the time – Durrus, Gubbeen and Ardrahan all appeared, each with a strong character. Funnily enough, some Irish cheesemakers believe it was early medieval Irish monks on a mission to the continent who taught the French how to make washed-rind cheeses in the first place. According to proponents of this theory, the most venerable of washed-rinds, the Alsatian Munster, is actually named for the Irish kingdom of Munster, of which County Cork was a part.

If that were the case, it is a pleasing symmetry that the 1970s cheesemakers on this side of the Channel were inspired by French washed-rinds. Alongside the troop of Cork cheeses, the 1980s Cheese Renaissance hero James Aldridge developed Tornegus, which as a washed Caerphilly is an inspiring example of how different cultures can collaborate fruitfully.

The renaissance, of course, has never really stopped, and new British and Irish washed-rind varieties appear all the time, including Edmund Tew, named for a convict transported for stealing cheese; Maida Vale, a washed version of Anne Wigmore's sheep cheese; and Highmoor, made on Ian Fleming's family estate. The most famous washed-rind in the British Isles, as much for its name as its qualities, must be the heavily aromatic Stinking Bishop, although a new kid on the block, the eye-watering blue/washed-rind hybrid, Renegade Monk, is snapping at its heels.

# Admiral Collingwood

## Made by Maggie Maxwell in Northumberland

UNPASTEURISED COW'S MILK, ANIMAL RENNET

Admiral Collingwood was a heroic Northumberland sailor who, under Nelson's command, led a line of ships into battle at Trafalgar. His cheese, aptly, is washed in another Northumberland icon, Newcastle Brown Ale, which perhaps helps give it a mild and complex character. The aroma on the rind has an animal warmth, a hint of mould and a slight ammoniac tang like the the straw bedding in a cow barn, and the paste has a light buttery scent. The texture is firm, almost like Cheddar, and there is also a Cheddary bite to the flavour, which begins mildly and develops heft, and a yeasty savouriness like the lees in a wooden beer barrel.

The Admiral is mild for a washed-rind, which may be down to the fact that the cheeses are allowed to mature and develop flavour for six months before being washed, in order to develop their *B. linens* rind. Their character is quite different from Maggie Maxwell's other cheeses, a fact she attributes to their maturation in a smaller, more moist store. She created this cheese not to fill a gap in the market but because she had always loved the Scottish washed-rind Criffel, now sadly no more. 'Make something you believe in and want to eat yourself,' she declares.

# Baronet

## Made by Julianna Sedli and Karim Niazy in Wiltshire

PASTEURISED COW'S MILK, ANIMAL RENNET

Baronet has a pillowy, quilted effect that, with its rosy colour, makes it look like a shiny pink overstuffed sofa. The paste has the rich buttery colour of Jersey milk, with a creamy breakdown and a hint of firmness in the centre, and the aroma shows a gentle note of fresh yeast and a trace of summer cow barn. The Jersey milk gives a lovely unctuous texture balanced with gentle acidity and a flavour of clean straw, finishing on freshly baked bread.

The delicacy and balance of this cheese is a product of Julianna Sedli's philosophy of cheesemaking, which is to add as little as possible. 'What's in the milk should come out,' she says. Julianna's cheesemaking journey is quite complex: she is from arable farming stock in Hungary and interned on a goat farm in Indiana before coming to England, where, in the cellars of Neal's Yard Dairy, she met Mary Holbrook – another hero of the Cheese Renaissance – and found herself working on Mary's farm. She spent two years there and, as she says, 'If you work with Mary you develop your personality, learn who you are and where you stand.' It was almost as if she was describing her own cheese.

# Drewi Sant

## Made by the Jennings family in Pembrokeshire

🐄 PASTEURISED COW'S MILK, VEGETARIAN RENNET

The Jennings family began farming in 1983, making them early players in the Cheese Renaissance. They had just returned from Libya and North Yemen, where they had been helping to set up dairying businesses, so it's not surprising that their cheeses are particularly distinctive.

Drewi Sant is washed in mead, which is not that out of the ordinary, as many great cheeses – like Époisses and Langres – are washed in booze. What is different about this cheese is how mild it is and how little it shows some of the flavours I'd expect from a cheese of this style. The aroma has the honeyed booziness of the mead, with a yeasty note like that of spent brewer's mash, but there was none of the farmy whiff so common to washed-rinds. The texture is creamy but still firm, and the flavour yoghurty and fresh with a light yeasty note ending on a grapey finish, which may come from the mead (though I also find it in one other washed-rind, the Alsatian Munster). I think this is less about youth than about how few times this cheese has been washed, and as a conscious decision represents a distinctive and very successful method of *affinage*.

# Durrus

## Made by Jeffa Gill in County Cork

🐾 PASTEURISED COW'S MILK, ANIMAL RENNET

The wet and salty climate of County Cork is perfect for washed-rinds and the county is well supplied with them, which is fine by me as I could happily consume a cheeseboard made up entirely of these cheeses. Durrus, even when aged, is a fairly restrained member of this boisterous family. The rinds are thin and only slightly moist – a thicker sticky rind usually denotes a more powerful cheese – and the texture is creamy, but not liquid like a Stinking Bishop. The washed-rind flavour that in polite society I describe as 'barnyardy' is present, but very much in moderation.

Young Durri – for that is the plural I have just invented – have notes of hay, and older ones become more earthy, but so far I have not found one that reaches the extremes of a cheese like Époisse. Jeffa also makes a smoked version. As a novice monger, with all the zeal of the newly converted, I was against smoking cheese, but I have softened with age, and I think a smoky, earthy Durrus with a hint of bacon would be a blessing to the world.

# Edmund Tew

## Made by Dave Holton and his team in Kent

UNPASTEURISED COW'S MILK, ANIMAL RENNET

Dave, who is originally from Australia, names his cheeses for convicts who were transported for stealing cheese – a category so large it makes me think that quality cheese might have been valued more highly back then than it is now. Dave and his cheese embody the sort of promiscuous hybridisation that characterises the later stages of the Cheese Renaissance. He began making a Feta-style cheese in Australia from a Persian recipe, before rumours of Neal's Yard Dairy led him to London, where he found himself working as an *affineur*. Starting out on the low-maintenance hard cheeses, which only really require a bit of rubbing and turning, it was when he moved to more demanding soft cheeses that his interest in cheesemaking was really piqued. He seems to relish a challenge, saying that what he likes about Edmund Tew is that 'it's a tricky make and tricky to mature as well.'

The cheese is a lactic style, made in a day rather than the usual twenty-four hours, and the faster make results in a lower acidity. Edmund Tew's are pudgy wrinkled little things, pink from their washing, with a hint of the funky flavour of that style that contrasts with their firmer zesty centre.

# Eve

## Made by Roger Longman and his team in Somerset

✿ UNPASTEURISED GOAT'S MILK, ANIMAL RENNET

Made from goat's milk, wrapped in a vine leaf, its rind washed in Somerset cider brandy, there's a lot going on with Roger Longman's Eve cheese. Neatly wrapped in its dark green leaf, it looks like a present from the elves, and the aroma of the vine leaf is predominant. As the luxuriant paste fills the mouth, the first flavour is goaty, but not overwhelmingly so. A slight ammoniac sting is all I get from the washing, which has left little but a golden sheen on the rind – the cheeses are washed only once during their maturation for a gentle effect. The flavour is balanced, with sweetness and a ghostly trace of volatile apple from the brandy. Goatiness is present from start to finish but tactfully interwoven with the other flavours, and the finish is sweet, with an edge of ammonia and a final hint of the brandy.

I tend to be a fan of simplicity in cheesemaking; the magic is in the complexity that can be derived from the four fundamental ingredients. For Eve, the cheesemaker's skill is apparent in how seamlessly all the different elements of this cheese work together to create a harmonious whole.

# Gubbeen

## Made by Giana Ferguson in County Cork

PASTEURISED COW'S MILK, VEGETARIAN RENNET

Continuing our tour of the washed-rinds of County Cork, this cheese is the mild-mannered scion of the family. *Gubbeen* means 'little mouthful', which is funny because I like to eat this cheese in big mouthfuls. It has a very springy texture, bouncy even, and when young, a blushing pink rind and a floral sweetness with just a hint of smoky bacon – think American breakfasts with bacon and maple syrup. Older cheeses develop a grey coat of mould, become firmer and show more mushroom and meaty flavours. Its mildness makes Gubbeen an excellent breakfast cheese, and if I am feeling the need for a stronger flavour I might toast it with some sort of garlicky pickle.

Giana Ferguson's background is as eccentric as any modern renaissance cheesemaker: she is Anglo-Hungarian by way of Spain, where she made goat's cheese on a farm as a child. Her husband's family have farmed the land for generations, and in traditional fashion, the whey from the cheesemaking is fed to pigs, who produce charcuterie flavoured with herbs from their market garden. In its interdependence and concern for sustainability, this system is probably as old as farming itself.

# Highmoor

## Made by Rose Grimond and her team in Oxfordshire

 PASTEURISED COW'S MILK, ANIMAL RENNET

We've met Rose Grimond before – the one-time actress making fine mould-ripened cheese (Bix and Witheridge) on her great-uncle Ian Fleming's Nettlebed estate. This plump square washed-rind is up to those standards.

Highmoor looks like a faded Roman roof tile and has an exciting stickiness that in a washed-rind usually indicates a fair bit of oomph in the flavour. The aroma of that rind has notes of beer, damp thatch and vinyl, reminiscent of the Wellington boot cupboard in a farmhouse.

The paste is a very pale yellow dotted with oval eyes and pinholes and has an aroma of just-turning sour cream. The stickiness on the rind deceived me – this cheese is delicate, yet marvellously complex with notes of wildflowers, butter, earth, and ending with a hint of white chocolate. Rather than intertwining, the different flavour notes emerge one after another. I often talk about the narrative structure of flavour in cheese, but this one has a well-constructed plot.

# Lindum

## Made by the Davenport family in Lincolnshire

 UNPASTEURISED COW'S MILK, ANIMAL RENNET

There's a lot of history going on with this cheese. Lindum was the Roman name for Lincoln, and the rind is washed in an ale called Bomber Country, which alludes to the Second World War role of Lincolnshire. Also, I'm quite sure that washed-rind cheeses were made in the medieval monasteries of Britain and Ireland, until Henry VIII got rid of them all (the monasteries that is), although the demise of washed-rinds must have followed. The rind is a happy orange-pink colour with the odd pockmark of blue on the sides showing a diverse upbringing. The aroma is busy with meaty barnyardy flavours, and the springy textured paste delivers notes of freshly stacked hay, 1970s grape juice soda and a long buttery finish. As often with washed-rinds, the flavour is mild for such a fulsome aroma. It's always exciting to wash cheeses and see the magical transformation effected by this method of *affinage*, and it's tempting to carry on washing until the cheese is as rambunctious as a French Époisses. The Davenports have resisted this temptation, washing Lindums only once every couple of days and sending them out at only eight weeks old, such that the flavour shows a restraint as elegant as their *affinage*.

# Little Rollright

## Made by David Jowett in Gloucestershire

🐄 PASTEURISED COW'S MILK, ANIMAL RENNET

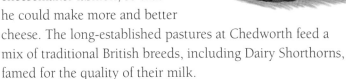

The Rollright Stones are a collection of prehistoric monuments near the Oxfordshire farm where David Jowett set up his first dairy. In 2019 he moved to Chedworth Farm in Gloucestershire, in true cheesemaker fashion, so that he could make more and better cheese. The long-established pastures at Chedworth feed a mix of traditional British breeds, including Dairy Shorthorns, famed for the quality of their milk.

Unlike its big sister, Rollright, which owes more to the French Reblochon, Little Rollright is bound in spruce like the Alpine Vacherin. The rind is a delicate rose pink, with a pretty dusting of *Penicillium camemberti* making for a startlingly beautiful cheese. The aroma has a volatile petrolly note with none of the wilder scents you'd expect in a washed-rind, and the flavour is very clean, the *B. linens* imparting gentle savoury and meaty notes, with no trace of the barnyard. A phenolic note of spruce tones up the rich creamy flavour and the salting is apparent but perfectly balanced. Like Vacherin, the paste is so liquid that, once you open the cheese, your best option is to eat it all at once. With such a complex, nuanced and perfectly balanced cheese, this is no hardship.

# Maida Vale

## Made by Anne and Andy Wigmore in Berkshire

UNPASTEURISED COW'S MILK, VEGETARIAN RENNET

At around an inch high and five across, Maida Vale cheeses are much the same shape as a Camembert. Their pink rinds are covered in a rich secondary growth of *Penicillium candidum* and look like snow covered roof tiles, with a bold whiff of ammonia and a hint of old books. The paste has the warm yellow of Guernsey milk and some well-developed eyes that promise a propionic sweetness. Notes of grass, hay and Colman's mustard are delivered by a delightfully giving creamy texture, and then from the middle flavour building to a triumphant finish is a resinous note such that I looked for a spruce band around the cheese. There is no band and actually the flavour is much more akin to cedar than spruce, with a hint of high-church incense. It is washed in Treason IPA by Uprising Brewery, an American West Coast style of intense hoppiness, whose strong resinous notes might account for that cedar flavour.

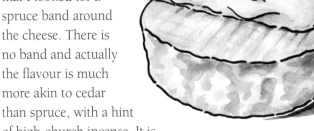

As with Ann Wigmore's other cheeses – Spenwood and Wigmore – Maida Vale shows a Continental influence, which is unsurprising given that she is one of the great cheesemakers of the British Cheese Renaissance.

# Merry Wyfe of Bath

## Made by Hugh Padfield and his team in Somerset

PASTEURISED COW'S MILK, ANIMAL RENNET

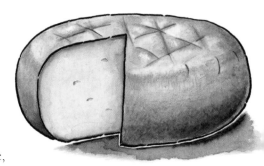

To make a Wyfe of Bath merry you wash the young cheese in cider every two days. The rind, a terracotta colour like an old roof tile, is pleasingly sticky with a dusting of naturally occurring crystallised tyrosine, suggesting tasty umami flavours in the cheese. The paste is firm but retains an unctuous texture, possibly the result of gentle pasteurisation – the milk sits for half an hour at 63°C rather than being rushed through a pasteuriser – patience and gentleness are both virtues in a cheesemaker. Buttery and sweet flavours – like uncooked crumble dough – develop a savoury note that, combined with the crumble flavour, reminds me of Twiglets. The finish is long for such a subtle cheese and, reminding you of its washed-rind status, ends on a slightly barnyardy note.

Merry Wyfe is actually the result of a competition. Hugh Padfield had been finding too many experimental cheeses lurking in the store and, deciding it was time to focus on one, called an anonymous ballot which a washed-rind Wyfe of Bath won. For the name, we can thank their herdsman, Josh, who said, 'You should call her tipsy, or merry, cos she's had a drink, hasn't she?'

# Milleens

## Made by Quinlan Steele in County Cork

 PASTEURISED COW'S MILK, ANIMAL RENNET

Of the County Cork washed-rinds, Milleens is, at time of writing, the heftiest. Its pink sticky rind and barnyardy aroma promise delights to come, and the texture of the paste is unctuously creamy, like a very ripe Brie. Flavours include any or all of the following: barnyard, smoky bacon, hay, hot tarmac, white chocolate, earth – truly, a cheese of character.

Quinlan Steele's mother, Veronica, began making cheese in the late 1970s, partly to use up excess milk from their one-horned cow, Brisket, and partly I suspect out of sheer curiosity – a useful trait in a cheesemaker. Another motive might have been that there wasn't that much interesting cheese around in Ireland at the time, so, just as in the UK, people started making their own. At first Milleens might have been a little bit too interesting for a national palate used to the unchallenging flavour profile of factory block cheese, but a chance encounter between the cheese and Michelin-starred chef Declan Ryan signalled a change in its fortunes. Over the next decade, Milleens, along with other Irish Renaiassance cheeses, took their rightful place as national cultural treasures.

# Ogleshield

## Made by Jamie Montgomery and Tim Giffey in Somerset

🐾 PASTEURISED COW'S MILK, ANIMAL RENNET

Ogleshield has an orange and blushing pink rind, and the paste has the warm golden colour of Jersey milk. To the touch, a fresh piece will have a light stickiness on the rind. The flavours are mild, with notes of fresh hay, sweet cream, a brothy savouriness and just a hint of that funky barnyard to remind you which family this cheese is from.

Ogleshield really comes into its own when you cook it, as the cheese is inspired by Raclette, which is both an Alpine cheese and a dish, in which that funky pink cheese is melted, scraped onto a pile of boiled new potatoes and served with gherkins. If you don't feel like making the effort, Ogleshield also makes brilliant cheese on toast.

Ogleshield started out as plain old Shield, made from the milk of Jamie's Jersey herd, which is not suited for Cheddar, and was so called because it looked like a Bronze Age shield that had been dug up nearby. Bill Oglethorpe, head *affineur* of Neal's Yard Dairy in the early-noughties, began washing the young Shields before they had developed their mould rinds, effectively creating a new cheese, which Jamie, to honour his contribution, opted to call Ogleshield.

# Oxford Isis

## Made in Alsace, France, then matured by Baron Roger Pouget in Oxfordshire

🐄 PASTEURISED COW'S MILK, VEGETARIAN RENNET

The enticingly sticky pink rind of this mead-washed cheese has an aroma of fresh yeast with just a trace of barnyard. The paste is well broken down with a faint trace of the firmer 'soul' in the centre. Opening innocuously with a sweet milk flavour, a hefty note of the barnyard comes shouldering through and, following on from the aroma, a strong taste of fresh yeast as if you'd bitten into a chunk. I suspect the mead has a hand in all this, and that the residual sugar in that honey-based medieval tipple has given the B. linens and other microorganisms a massive sugar high so that they are running wild like kids in a playground. The flavours end in a big floral finish, not that of gentle meadow flowers but something more heady and blowsy, like orchids in a fin de siècle courtesan's boudoir.

As with the Baron's other cheese, Oxford Blue, this is made by someone else – in this case a Munster producer in the Alsace region of France. The cheeses arrive in Oxfordshire young, firm and white but are then washed in mead brewed in Somerset. This is a cheese with a double terroir.

# Rachel

## Made by Roger Longman and his team in Somerset

 UNPASTEURISED GOAT'S MILK, VEGETARIAN RENNET

These flying-saucer-shaped Rachel cheeses have a terracotta rind and a nobbled surface from the cheese moulds. The paste is dense, perfectly uniform, with a rich ivory colour more like sheep's milk than goat's. The recipe is based on a Gouda style and includes the washing of the curd, which accounts for the dense texture of the paste and the sweet flavour.

Roger Longman's mistrust of curd-washing is trumped by another fundamental principle of cheesemaking – don't mess with something when it's good. When freshly cut, the cheese itself gives a lovely foresty aroma of acorns, and overall there is a malty sweetness with just a hint of goat, and as the firm texture breaks down in the mouth the intensity builds, leaving a long tail of piquant spice in the finish. You also feel that with every mouthful (and I have had quite a few) different flavours come through.

Like so many cheese styles, Rachel in its current form came about by accident. The original cheeses grew a coat of an undesirable mould called *mucor*, which can be treated with brine-washing. *B. linens* moved in and, the result being so tasty, the rind-washing stuck.

# Renegade Monk

## Made by Marcus Fergusson in Somerset

🐄 PASTEURISED COW'S MILK, VEGETARIAN RENNET

Traditional cheeses evolve, often over centuries. It's not as if a medieval cheesemaker sat down with a bit of paper and said, 'I'm going to design a new cheese, hard, in a cylinder about a foot high, with a beefy flavour. We'll call it Cheddar.'

For contemporary cheesemakers setting up a new business, developing a cheese is a more conscious process, and in Marcus Fergusson's case eminently so. Having moved to the heart of Cheddar country, he decided quite sensibly not to go up against centuries of experience and tradition by producing another one. Seeing that the market lacked niches, he decided to create one, the nichiest niche there could be – indeed, a novel family of cheese – the washed-rind blue. In Renegade Monk, the barnyardy flavour of a washed-rind is egged on by the piquant flavour of blue cheese, served up to the palate in an indulgently creamy paste.

The name does some heavy lifting for two words: Monk alludes to the monastic origins of washed-rinds; Renegade to the non-canonical addition of the blue. Furthermore, Marcus's farm is near Templecombe, once an outpost of the Templars, the original Renegade Monks.

# Saint Cera

## Made by Julie Cheyney in Suffolk

UNPASTEURISED COW'S MILK, ANIMAL RENNET

Nothing illustrates the magically transformative powers of washing better than Saint Cera – the washed-rind sibling of Julie Cheyney's Saint Jude. Merely by the repeated application of brine plus a lot of loving care and attention, the firm-fudgey, delicately flavoured Saint Jude becomes a cheese so liquid that it needs to be delivered in a box, and once opened usually demands to be eaten in one go.

This is a cheese with considerable character, opening with a yeasty aroma so lively it's like smelling a still-fermenting ale, and delivering a meaty, salty and savoury suite of flavours best accompanied with equally authoritative drinks like a big, fulsome Burgundy, a rich dark stout or a peaty Islay single malt.

In a crowded field, Julie is one of the nicest cheesemakers I have ever met. Growing up on a dairy farm she had always been enticed by the magic and glamour of cheesemaking, saying to me with great satisfaction after a hard day's ladling, 'I'm the dairymaid who grew up to be a cheesemaker.'

# Saint James

## Made by Martin Gott and his team in Cumbria

UNPASTEURISED SHEEP'S MILK, ANIMAL RENNET

This is another cheese named after a saint, but in this instance a secular one – James Aldridge, hero monger of the Cheese Renaissance, who popularised artisan cheese in the 1980s and, as an *affineur*, developed new styles like the pillowy sheep's milk, Flower Marie. For Martin Gott, Aldridge wasn't merely a distant heroic figure; it was the maestro's visits to the Gott family's farm that set him on the path of cheesemaking.

Another reason for the saintly name might be the likely monastic origin of washed-rind cheeses. You might not think that washed-rinds and sheep's milk cheeses are traditional British families. But given that (until Henry VIII got rid of them) monastic houses, using milk from their huge flocks of sheep, dominated British and Irish cheesemaking, I believe Saint James is one of our most traditional-style cheeses.

Unlike many washed-rinds, I find Saint James to have a mild flavour, floral with a hint of yeast and a lovely silky paste from the rich sheep's milk. Cheese being cheese, though, some batches of Saint James will be much more raucous, with that barnyardy note and even perhaps a hint of smoke that we expect from the washed-rind family. That's the fun of it, right?

# Saval

## Made by John Savage-Onstwedder and his team in Ceredigion

🐾 UNPASTEURISED COW'S MILK, ANIMAL RENNET

With its plumply hatched surface, where the wire racks have left their mark, and the peachy terracotta shade of the rind, Saval is a very attractive cheese. The texture of the paste is creamy yet firm and, although there is no breakdown, the cheese has ripened thoroughly – there is a firm yet creamy texture all the way to the centre. Opening with a pronounced whiff of the farm, the first flavour I pick up is sweetness, opening out into white chocolate with a trace of estery fruitiness, finishing on a tingling acidity.

John Savage-Onstwedder began cheesemaking on his Welsh farm in 1981, and is a significant figure in the country's artisan cheese movement. Embodying the cross-cultural fertilisation of the Cheese Renaissance, he came over from the Netherlands and brought Dutch cheesemaking methods with him, along with a lovely traditional teak vat. Saval is a living example of this cheese multiculturalism, combining a traditional Caerphilly recipe with the continental practice of rind-washing.

# Stinking Bishop

## Made by Charles Martell in Gloucestershire

PASTEURISED COW'S MILK, VEGETARIAN RENNET

Stinking Bishop was voted Britain's smelliest cheese at the Royal Bath and West Show in 2009 – but that is not the only interesting thing about this cheese. For one thing, the name refers to an historical personage, and not the distinctive bouquet.

Frederick Bishop was a nineteenth-century Gloucestershire farmer whose legendary unpopularity was commemorated in the name of a local variety of pear – Stinking Bishop.

Martell washes the cheeses in a perry made from Stinking Bishop pears to give them their oozing texture and controversial aroma. If you feel a bit put off by the pungency, try to get past it – like many washed-rinds, the Bishop's bark is worse than his bite, and the flavour less intense than you might expect.

Martell began making cheese in the early 1970s to revive the near-extinct local breed of Gloucester cows. Having saved a breed, he then went on to save a style of cheese, the less well-known sibling of Double Gloucester, Single Gloucester, which received protected domain status in 1994, enshrining its status as a unique Gloucestershire product. So, when you eat some Stinking Bishop you can feel proud that you are helping to preserve British dairying culture.

# Westray Wife

## Made by Jason and Nina Wilson on Orkney

 PASTEURISED COW'S MILK, VEGETARIAN RENNET

Surprisingly, the climate of the Orkney islands is temperate due to the proximity of the Gulf Stream, resulting in lush pastures and excellent milk. The Wilsons sow a rich variety of grasses and herbs that give their Ayrshire cows – whose milk is already rich and creamy – a healthy varied diet and add to the quality of the milk and complexity of the cheese. Westray is based on Alpine styles like Raclette or Morbier, and a sign of this cheese's cultural roots is its pink washed-rind, which adds some funk to the flavour.

Small production means much of the cheese is sold young, but that's okay – at three months this is already a smashing cheese. The texture is actually bouncy, and there is a flavour like the dough for apple crumble, a biscuit mix of butter, flour and sugar with a salty finish that adds contrast. Delightful on a cheeseboard, a young Westray would really sing if used to make melted cheese dishes like *Raclette* or *Tartiflette*. If one were lucky enough to bag an older piece, it would have all the profundity and intensity of its Alpine forebears.

# Semi-soft cheeses

# Semi-soft cheeses

Caerfai Caerffili . . . . . . . . . . .132

Carlow Farmhouse . . . . . . . .133

Cornish Yarg . . . . . . . . . . . .134

Crookwheel . . . . . . . . . . . . .135

Crump's Single
Gloucester . . . . . . . . . . . . . .136

Cuddy's Cave . . . . . . . . . . . .137

Duckett's Caerphilly . . . . . . .138

Dunmanus . . . . . . . . . . . . . .139

Fellstone (Whin Yeats
Wensleydale) . . . . . . . . . . . .140

Gorwydd Caerphilly . . . . . . .141

Martell's Single Gloucester . .142

Monkland . . . . . . . . . . . . . .143

Moorland Tomme . . . . . . . . .144

Old Roan . . . . . . . . . . . . . . .145

Rainton Tomme . . . . . . . . . .146

Richard III Wensleydale . . . .147

Rockfield . . . . . . . . . . . . . . .148

Seator's Orkney . . . . . . . . . .149

Stonebeck Wensleydale . . . . .150

Stoney Cross . . . . . . . . . . . .151

Suffolk Gold . . . . . . . . . . . .152

Thelma's Caerffili . . . . . . . . .153

Ticklemore . . . . . . . . . . . . . .154

Wiltshire Loaf . . . . . . . . . . . .155

Yorkshire Pecorino . . . . . . . .156

# Semi-soft cheeses

Semi-soft is a hard to define category. For me, it means cheeses that have a bit of body, and can be sliced, but are softer and less dense than classic hard cheeses like Cheddar or Cheshire. You would struggle to spread a semi-soft cheese on a cracker without breaking it. Some cheesemongers describe washed-rinds as semi-soft. This makes sense to me for cheeses like the springy-textured Gubbeen, but I can't imagine anyone calling a fully ripe and virtually liquid Stinking Bishop semi-soft, so for the sake of clarity I have kept washed-rinds apart in their own section.

As befits a rather fuzzy category, there are no specific methods for making a semi-soft cheese, but on the whole the curd is heated to a lower temperature and cut to a larger particle size than for hard cheeses. I would describe most semi-soft cheeses as pressed, uncooked curd cheeses, though this depends on your definition of 'cooked'. Anthony Heard, who makes a Cypriot-style Halloumi in his London dairy, is very specific. It's 38°C, the point at which he can see the curd change before his eyes. For Cumbrian sheep's cheesemaker Martin Gott, any heating above the temperature of renneting – the low 20s°C – is cooking the curd. Strictest of all is Julie Cheyney, maker of the fudgey Saint Jude in Suffolk, who suggests that anything over the natural temperature of milk from the cow constitutes cooking. Leonie Fairbairn, who makes a range of cow's and goat's milk cheeses near Carlisle, also points out that the different milks behave quite differently and the cooking temperature for goat's cheese is lower than that for cows. Even if the method of cooking and cutting the curd would usually result in a hard cheese, what happens afterwards in the cellar can be enough to shift it into my semi-soft category. Wiltshire cheese Stoney Cross is made to the same recipe as its hard stablemate Old Winchester, but then ladled into smaller moulds and matured for a shorter time, resulting in a softer more open texture.

So that's clear enough. However, some types of cheese can be both hard and semi-soft. Wensleydale is a classic example. Pre-war farmhouse Wensleydale was softer and creamier than its modern counterpart, and often known as Pickled Wensleydale for its time in a brine bath. It was hand-made from raw milk on farms high up in the dale, and was so open-textured that many cheeses blued and were highly prized for it. Unfortunately, when the Second World War led to rationing, it was too soft to cut into the tiny pieces, and officials from the Ministry of Food were ready to close down cheesemaking in the Yorkshire Dales when Kit Calvert stepped in and persuaded his fellow producers to change to a harder, more acidic recipe. Many of the women who made a creamy Wensleydale on their farms gave up in disgust, and not long after the end of the war old-style farmhouse Wensleydale had all but disappeared.

Post-war Wensleydale is exemplified by cheeses made at Hawes Creamery, high up in the dale itself. My favourite is a cloth-bound, animal-rennet cheese which is actually called Kit Calvert, firm textured, fresh tasting and eminently sessionable. It is a lovely cheese, which I have put in the hard cheese section of this book. Happily, though, in the last few years some pre-war style Wensleydales have appeared phoenix-like from the ashes. By researching old recipes, and in one case talking to a Mrs Peacock who at 101 may have been at the time the last surviving pre-war maker, some cheesemakers have resurrected the old style, and you will find their creamy, delicate yet complex cheeses – Old Roan, Richard III, Stonebeck, and Whin Yeats (or Fellstone) – in this chapter.

Although you will find some continental-inspired cheeses like Yorkshire Pecorino in this chapter, I think of semi-soft as very much a traditional British style, and several of the following cheeses are what we mongers refer to as 'territorials' – cheeses with a long history and heritage, closely associated with certain counties. This is down to certain accidents of history and geography. Farmhouse cheesemaking really got off the ground, in Britain at least, in the seventeenth century, when the new class of yeoman farmers needed to produce commodities to pay the rent to their aristocratic landlords. A Cheddar needs at least a year to reach its potential, whereas a cheese like Caerphilly could be ready in a week or two. Therefore, fast-ripening semi-soft cheeses would have offered a quicker return on investment than hard cheeses, providing more liquidity, if you will, while still being hard enough to survive the bumpy trip to market in an unsprung cart.

Few cheesemakers in seventeenth-century Britain or Ireland were much more than a day's trip from a market, and so their cheeses didn't need to be as durable than those of, say, the Alpine cheesemakers who had to get down off an Alp before starting the journey to a market. So, in Britain and Ireland, for its taste – not too intense, not too mild, wonderfully complex – semi-soft cheese was a Goldilocks cheese of practicality and flavour and became a glorious part of our food heritage.

# Caerfai Caerffili

## Made by Linda Evans in Pembrokeshire

PASTEURISED COW'S MILK, ANIMAL RENNET

This Welsh-made (and spelled) Caerphilly cheese has a bright sunny yellow colour, firm moist crumble, and gentle lemony acidity, stiffened with a steely mineral edge. Overall the flavour is fresh, simple and gentle, with a buttery finish to round things out.

Caerfai is sold at two weeks, when it retains these qualities, although the family do age some to one or two months, when the rind starts to show some mould growth and the cheese beings to break down. The difference between young cheese like this and older Caerphillies with a thick growth of rind and substantial breakdown is such that they might almost be two different cheeses. When I sold Gorwydd, an example of the latter, some people refused to recognise it as Caerphilly.

Venerated Welsh cheese teacher Eurwen Richards reckons that traditionally 'most people wanted a cheese to eat on the farm and would have eaten it at two to three weeks', although she allows that some of it might have sat in the cellar for longer and developed that rind. I asked Todd Trethowan, who makes Gorwydd, if he thought his was 'proper' Caerphilly, to which he replied, 'I don't know, fella. It's just the cheese I make on my farm.'

# Carlow Farmhouse

## Made by Elizabeth Bradley in County Carlow

THERMISED COW'S MILK, ANIMAL RENNET

The rind of Carlow Farmhouse has a pattern of fine hatching on it, the imprint of the cloths that wrapped it as it sat draining in the mould. The paste is quite pale, with a scattering of small holes, and gives off a gentle floral aroma reminiscent of cow parsley. The soft springy texture melts swiftly in the mouth, coating the palate in a sumptuous way, a result of the gentle heating that the milk has been subjected too, hence 'thermised' rather than 'pasteurised'. I get a sweet cream flavour followed by umami, earth and an evocative grassy note as of summer pasture after a brief rain shower.

Elizabeth Bradley, who has farmed for most of her life, studied cheesemaking in Ireland and the Haute-Savoie in France, a continental influence that shows in this cheese, which she describes as an 'Edam style' – it's vastly superior to any Edam I've ever tried – and a goat's milk Tomme.

Elizabeth also makes a traditional Cheddar, of which she says that it 'brought people's minds back to what they used to have available', back when some pubs would have a whole cloth-bound cheese on the bar to sell along with the pints of Guinness.

# Cornish Yarg

## Made by Catherine Mead and her team in Cornwall

PASTEURISED COW'S MILK, VEGETARIAN RENNET

Cornish Yarg is a strong contender for the world's most beautiful cheese, especially when young and the nettles that cover it in their ferny tessellated patterns are still a deep forest green. The recipe is similar to that of a traditional Caerphilly, but the nettles prevent a mould rind from forming and breaking down the cheese. The result is a crumbly moist texture and a refreshing citrusy acidity.

When I first heard of this cheese I thought 'Yarg' was a word in some West Country dialect, then I discovered it is the cheesemaker's name spelt backwards. Alan Gray from Bodmin Moor started making the cheese in the 1970s. It is said that Mr Gray found a seventeenth-century recipe in the attic, which may have been in Gervase Markham's *English Huswife*, published in 1615, suggesting a pedigree of four hundred years or so. Furthermore, the use of nettles in cheesemaking goes back at least to Roman times and, since they were over here for a while, perhaps the recipe shows an influence, giving Yarg a pedigree of more than 2,000 years.

The Meads also make the wonderful Cornish Kern, which is based on a Dutch Gouda recipe but uses Alpine starters for their nutty sweet flavour and Ayrshire milk for its richness.

# Crookwheel

## Made by Martin Gott and his team in Cumbria

UNPASTEURISED SHEEP'S MILK, ANIMAL RENNET

Crookwheel represents a departure for Martin Gott from his silky soft Saint James (see *Washed-rind cheeses*). Sheep give milk in the summer, and being soft and short-lived there wasn't much Saint James around at Christmastime, which is not ideal in the busiest season. The plan to make a longer-keeping cheese gained considerable impetus when the closure of restaurants in the 2020 Covid lockdown left Martin with a store full of soft cheese and little outlet for it.

Necessity has been the mother of many new cheese styles, and Crookwheel is no less excellent for having been born out of a challenging economic situation. It's a pretty cheese to look at. The wrinkly mould rind is grey-blue with a dusting of white and light terracotta and has an engraved look from the lines the drying racks have left on it, like a shard from a millstone. The paste has a springy texture, in the younger batches, and a creamy breakdown around the edge. The flavour is clean with notes of freshly cut wood, country church and, rather marvellously, the sweet milky flavour of milk-bottle sweets. Finally, the earthy rind with a slight ammoniac tang adds depth of character to this balanced complex cheese.

# Crump's Single Gloucester

## Made by Jonathan Crump in Gloucester

 UNPASTEURISED COW'S MILK, VEGETARIAN RENNET

The rind of a Crump's Single Gloucester shows only a light dusting of blue-grey mould, but it still makes its own contribution to the flavour profile. The paste has an aroma of late summer meadows, thistle flowers and a yoghurty tang.

The texture is firm but melting, and delivers a burst of fresh cream and yoghurty freshness. Notes of earth and cellar finish with a trace of butter and minerality and long tail of zingy acidity.

Jonathan Crump got into farming for a love of rare breeds which began in child-hood, when he liked to look at pictures of dairy cows in books. Starting off with the Irish Kerry, he soon fell in love with the Gloucester breed for their beauty, and because they are unique, untainted by the 'improvements' of nineteenth-century cattle breeders – the quote marks are Crump's, apparent in his tone of voice. A compelling reason for a cheesemaker to use a traditional local cow is that, historically, individual breeds evolved to make best use of their particular *terroir*. In 1999 Jonathan began making cheese with the milk from his eight cows after a single lesson from Val Bines. He now has twenty cows, and last year sent Val some of his cheese as a twenty-first-anniversary gift.

# Cuddy's Cave

## Made by Maggie Maxwell in Northumberland

UNPASTEURISED COW'S MILK, ANIMAL RENNET

Cuddy's Cave is named after a local Northumbrian rock feature in which wandering monks briefly hid their holy relic, the body of Saint Cuthbert. Cuthbert was a celebrated miracle worker, talking to crows, healing the sick and stopping a storm by getting some monks to cook a goose. There's something miraculous about this cheese, too: it manages to be mild and intense at the same time. The rind has an aroma of damp canvas, reminding me of stowing wet sails, and the paste has an aroma of fresh yoghurt. At first I get tartness, developing into a mild note of red berries, a slight nuttiness and a broad milky flavour. The tartness builds up to a tingling level of acidity but unlike in many other cheeses stays just at that level rather than ramping up any further.

Cuddy's Cave is described as a Dales style cheese, for which the whey is drained off, and the curd is allowed to matt together and then milled. In the Dutch style, Maggie Maxwell takes the curd out of the whey and puts it straight into moulds, and as a result, unlike those light crumbly cheeses, Cuddy's Cave has a more supple texture.

# Duckett's Caerphilly

**Made by Tom Calver and his team in Somerset**

🐄 UNPASTEURISED COW'S MILK, ANIMAL RENNET

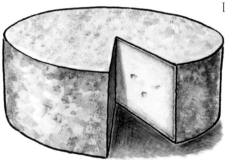

It is fascinating to me that two cheeses of the same style – Duckett's and Gorwydd Caerphillies – can be quite so different. Duckett's exhibits that moist crumbly centre, creamy breakdown and grey mushroomy rind which are typical characteristics of a farmhouse Caerphilly, but is firmer than Gorwydd. For me there is less of the acidity and more of the earth in its flavour profile.

While these differences could be down to *terroir*, that became less likely when Gorwydd moved from Wales to Somerset, and I think it is more to do with the cheesemaker's idiosyncrasies. When Chris Duckett was still making the cheese, Duckett's was firmer still, with barely any breakdown, which reflects the earlier history of his cheese. Before Neal's Yard Dairy started maturing Caerphilly until it had grown a rind, Duckett's was sold at a few weeks old, rindless, fresh and firm.

The existence of a traditional farmhouse Caerphilly in Somerset is a reminder of a moment in the cheese's history. In the nineteenth century, Cheddar makers waiting for return on their twelve-month matured Cheddar turned to making the odd batch of Caerphilly, a fast-maturing cheese they could sell at a few weeks old to generate some cash flow.

# Dunmanus

## Made by Jeffa Gill in County Cork

🐄 UNPASTEURISED COW'S MILK, ANIMAL RENNET

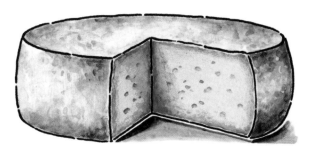

Dunmanus has a grey mould rind, like a sort of smooth Caerphilly. The earthy, mushroomy flavours and the firm yet creamy paste, with its dotting of small holes, are reminiscent of an Alpine Tomme. The family call it a table cheese for its versatility, making a meal in itself as a ploughman's lunch, or an ingredient in something more fancy, like a gratin.

Tommes are a relatively low-tech style. For example, the curd is pressed by hand into the moulds, so there's no need to splash out on fancy cast-iron cheese presses. Down to earth, yet versatile, this seems to me like the quintessential peasant cheese and as such might have been a style that Irish farmers made. Tragically we have to guess at what these might have been, since the ancient indigenous cheeses of Ireland are no more, made extinct by the cheese imperialism of the Norman and English colonists. On a happier note, the Cheese Renaissance initiated a flowering of artisan cheesemaking and, while the methods may be modern, or revived, the *terroir* can't have changed that much. I like to think an ancient cheesemaker catapulted forward in time would recognise the flavours and textures of Dunmanus.

# Fellstone (Whin Yeats Wensleydale)

## Made by Clare and Tom Noblet in Cumbria

🐄 UNPASTEURISED COW'S MILK, ANIMAL RENNET

There is a new movement afoot in the world of British cheese; it's called 'The Rise of the Territorials'. Well, I call it that, and I'm hoping it's going to catch on. Territorials are a mild and often crumbly style unique to Britain and, as more delicate cheeses, their reputation suffered much from less complex factory versions. Fellstone is part of this movement. Made to a recipe from 1933, it harks back to a time when Wensleydale was softer, creamier and made in farmhouses all over the Yorkshire Dales and beyond.

Wartime Wensleydales were made more acidic and harder, to fit in with the requirements of rationing, which is why Hawes, the product of a creamery rather than a farmhouse, is in the hard cheese category. One of the first farmhouse Wensleydales to appear on our cheeseboards for more than half a century, Fellstone is softer and smoother. Its pale colour and springy texture promise all the delight of a mild yet complex cheese. The gentle yoghurty tang fills out into a buttery flavour with notes of green herbs and the salt level is perfect, coming through clearly in the finish. Though mild, the flavour has length and draws me back for more. This is sessionable cheese.

# Gorwydd Caerphilly

## Made by the Trethowan brothers in Somerset

UNPASTEURISED COW'S MILK, ANIMAL RENNET

It was a taste of Gorwydd Caerphilly, my first proper cheese, one chilly winter morning at Borough Market, that set me on my way to becoming a cheesemonger. But that's not the only reason that this is one of my favourite cheeses. It was partly the realisation that a cheese doesn't have to be strong to be outstanding that fascinated me so much. That, and the way that a cheese, even though made  from the same four simple ingredients – milk, starter, rennet and salt – and to the same method, could change so much from batch to batch.

Above all this is the range of flavours and textures that makes this wonderful creation three cheeses in one. The bone-white centre of the cheese is moistly crumbly with a citrusy acidity, familiar to everyday Caerphilly fanciers, but this hand-made farmhouse-style cheese has more to it: the next layer (called the breakdown) is a richer yellow with a creamy texture and a peppery vegetal flavour reminiscent of Camembert. This texture and flavour are the result of the mould rind 'breaking down' the cheese. The rind, a cosy grey velvet coat, has its own flavour which shouldn't be missed: the cellary air of a nice old parish church.

# Martell's Single Gloucester

## Made by Charles Martell in Gloucestershire

 UNPASTEURISED COW'S MILK, ANIMAL RENNET

Martell's Single Gloucester has a velvety coat of grey mould pleasingly dappled with white, and the paste is a fresh yellow with a grassy aroma and a hint of mustiness from the rind. The cheese has a warm savoury flavour and summery notes of camomile lawns and hawthorn hedges, with a gentle acidity and a mineral finish.

Charles began cheesemaking in 1972, in large part to revive the all but extinct Gloucester cow. His affection for this local breed is infectious. 'They're magical to me,' he explains. 'The look of 'em, with their lovely upswept horns. They've got a mischief about them.' Luckily for Charles, the Gloucester's milk, high in protein and fat, is excellent for cheesemaking; the small fat globules mean it is naturally homogenised such that the fat doesn't rise to the top after renneting. In reviving the breed, Charles also revived another, fully extinct local treasure – Single Gloucester. Softer and more delicate than the more hardy and robustly flavoured Double, Single Gloucester 'never made it off the farm'. Faster ripening, and therefore losing less volume, it made a cheaper alternative to feed the labourers. We are lucky to be able to sample the subtle yet complex delights of this singular cheese.

# Monkland

## Made by Karen and Mark Hindle in Herefordshire

🐄 UNPASTEURISED COW'S MILK, ANIMAL RENNET

With its rounded edges, Monkland looks like a small plump Gouda, except instead of wax the cheese has a natural rind with a light dusting of blue and white moulds. The paste is surprisingly pale, almost white, the result of acidity leaching carotene out of the curd, and has a uniform texture with a scattering of small holes. The aroma is light with a hint of butter and a trace of mould. In the mouth the texture is firm with a moist crumble, and the flavour is clean and simple with a juicy acidity, a vein of minerality running through, and a surprising note of brown sugar. The finish is long, with a fresh juicy acidity that leaves my mouth watering for a while after.

That minerality and juicy acid remind me of Cheshire, which isn't surprising. After that cheese's meteoric rise to fame and fortune in the eighteenth century, cheeses of a similar style sprang up all over neighbouring counties. Unlike cloth-bound Cheshire, Monkland has a natural rind and the light dusting of mould adds a different character to the cheese. The holes signal a higher temperature make and the presence of propionic bacteria that accounts for that surprising sweetness in the finish.

# Moorland Tomme

## Made by Alastair Pearson and his team in North Yorkshire

UNPASTEURISED COW'S MILK, VEGETARIAN RENNET

A Moorland's rind is the colour of vellum, its gnarled surface ridged with the marks of the cheesecloths in which it has drained. It has an intriguing aroma, sweet, musty, slightly animal, while the paste itself has a note of caramel. Firm, yet moist, the texture is creamy and slightly springy, and the flavour, starting out sweet, develops a fresh grassy note, followed by a hint of the barnyard, and finally a long hot mustard finish.

Tommes are a family of cheeses often found in mountainous regions like the Auvergne or the Pyrenees, though the most widely known, Tomme de Savoie is from the French Alps. The name, which refers to a unit of cheese, like the British 'wheel' or 'truckle', may come from a Latin or Greek root meaning a cut, a slice, or pleasingly, part of a book. Tommes are traditionally made in the summer when the animals are grazing on the high pastures rich in flowers and herbs. It would be un-canonical to make a Tomme in winter from silage fed milk, and so Alastair makes Moorland only when the cows are grazing contentedly on the lush pastures of the Yorkshire moors.

# Old Roan

## Made by the Spence family in North Yorkshire

 UNPASTEURISED COW'S MILK, ANIMAL RENNET

As a traditional Wensleydale, Old Roan is a cloth-bound cheese, and its rind has a rumpled look where the cloth has gathered. These darker rivulets look like channels eroded into old stone, an appearance enhanced by the silvered look of the white mould. The pale paste shades to a darker shade around the edge as the rind acts on the cheese, breaking down the texture and adding complexity. There is a note of cucumber in the aroma and the flavour is mouthwatering – rich and savoury, with an earthy animal note from the rind.

Made with raw milk to a slow, low temperature recipe, Old Roan signifies a return to the traditional style of Wensleydale, so it is right and proper that the Spences are based at Aysgarth in the lower end of the dale. Harold and Norma Spence bought their farm and began milking their Dairy Shorthorn cows in 1953 shortly after their marriage, but four years later farmhouse Wensleydale would disappear from the national cheeseboard. Their grandsons Ben and Sam began making Old Roan in 2019 and, from the sight of a very small pair of wellies outside the cheese room door, the next generation is waiting in the wings.

# Rainton Tomme

## Made by Wilma and David Finlay and Stephen Palmer in Dumfries and Galloway

UNPASTEURISED COW'S MILK, VEGETARIAN RENNET

The rind of a Rainton Tomme has a terracotta colour and a pleasing leopard-print effect from the way the moulds have grown. Overall the flavour is mild, as you would expect from a Tomme style, but satisfyingly complex, opening with a hint of cow barn, developing a clean tropical fruit note, bringing the barn back for a bit, and finishing on a savoury toasted cheese flavour.

There's a fair bit of legacy in this cheese. Stephen Palmer's uncle was legendary Stilton maker Ernie Wagstaff, and he has obviously inherited the family knack for cheesemaking. David's uncle, who farmed nearby, was J. Brian Finlay, who in 1973 was given the farmhouse cheesemaking cup in perpetuity because there were no other cheesemakers left to compete with him (he himself stopped the following year). Having diversified from liquid milk to ice-cream production in the 1990s, David and Wilma Finlay decided to return to cheesemaking in 2008. Cheese is much tastier and more interesting than ice-cream (at least, *I* think so), also it can travel further afield, entering a larger market. David said this meant their cheese would have to be 'bloody good or at least have a unique story'. They seem to have nailed both criteria.

# Richard III Wensleydale

## Made by Andy Ridley in Lancashire

🐄 PASTEURISED COW'S MILK, VEGETARIAN RENNET

I was excited on unwrapping my first Richard III Wensleydale to see a mottling of blue on its rind, reminding me of a brindled cow. A narrow layer of breakdown told me that the rind had indeed been getting involved with the maturation of this cheese. The texture is springy and soft and the cheese melts as it warms in the mouth, a sprightly acidity giving way to a sweet finish.

Don't let the Ridleys' current home in Lancashire confuse you – Wensleydale is a style as much as a geographical indication. And Richard III has authenticity and pedigree enough for the most ardent traditionalist. The cheese, which was originally made by cheesemaker Susan Stirke from her grandmother's notes, which she found in the attic, is another example of a pre-war style recently brought back from extinction. Susan's dairy was not far from Middleham in Wensleydale, and it was this location that suggested a name for her cheese. The castle whose ruins still dominate this picturesque market town was the childhood home of Richard III.

# Rockfield

## Made by Michael Flanagan in County Mayo

🐑 PASTEURISED SHEEP'S MILK, ANIMAL RENNET

Rockfield has a light fawn rind with a scattering of white mould, giving the effect of a sheet of parchment onto which has fallen a light dusting of snow. The pale ivory paste has a crumbly appearance and a musty lemony smell, reminiscent of Caerphilly. In the mouth, the texture is an intriguing mix of crumble and flexibility, and the flavour opens on a fresh clean start, moving to a warm caramel centre with hints of candyfloss and delivering a rich lanolin flavour in the finish.

Michael Flanagan's family have been farming in County Mayo for generations, and he grew up milking cows and raising sheep, 'so I reckon I had a bit of a handle on both', he said modestly. Michael started 'messing about with cheesemaking' in 2016, working from a Pyrenean Ossau Iraty recipe. Wanting to make something softer than Ossau, his cheese, after a few years of experimentation and some less than perfect batches, has come into its own – softer and more crumbly than that mountain-style cheese. In 2019, Rockfield won a silver medal at the World Cheese Awards, the first competition he had entered, which shows that messing about is an entirely valid way to proceed in life, or indeed cheesemaking.

# Seator's Orkney

## Made by Anne Seator on Orkney

🐝 PASTEURISED COW'S MILK, VEGETARIAN RENNET

Orkney is famous for its collection of Neolithic remains, and monumental sites like the Ring of Brodgar still inspire awe. But it is the cosy little village of Skara Brae, built before the Great Pyramids, with its oddly familiar beds, dressers and hearths, that I find most moving. Its inhabitants were keen pastoralists, raising cattle and sheep, and since by then the people of the British Isles had been making cheese for almost a thousand years I find it hard to imagine that the people of Skara Brae were wasting all that lovely milk.

I think that Seator's was just the sort of cheese they would have made – Anne's mother Hilda used to make the cheese in an ancient way, in that she didn't use a starter culture but just let the milk sour naturally. Although Anne uses starter these days for consistency's sake, when young and rindless this clean, simple fresh-tasting cheese would be familiar to her Neolithic forebears. With its mild lactic tang and crumbly texture, a young Seator's pre-figures British favourites like Cheshire and Lancashire and as such I would also like to categorise it as an 'ur-territorial'.

# Stonebeck Wensleydale

## Made by Andrew and Sally Hattan in North Yorkshire

UNPASTEURISED COW'S MILK, ANIMAL RENNET

The rind of a Stonebeck Wensleydale has the rough texture of bark and the colour of limestone, and the paste gives off a cool green aroma of cress with a tinge of mustiness from the rind. Its texture is a singular combination of creaminess, moist crumble and a slight springiness, which softens in the mouth to deliver a lemony acidity and green notes of cress and clover like a summer meadow. There is a hint of buttery sweetness, and all through the flavour palette runs that juicy mouthwatering acidity.

The Hattans graze their Northern Dairy Shorthorns, a traditional local breed well suited to their *terroir*, on the meadowlands and pastures of Nidderdale, 900 feet above sea level. It's not surprising, then, that you find notes of summer meadow, particularly as Stonebeck is only made when the cows are out on those pastures. The cheese, with its soft open texture and gentle acidity, is a pre-war farmhouse style, and to make it the Hattans had to go back to recipes from the 1930s and talk to local cheesemaker Mrs Peacock, who at 101 was one of the few people left in the world who know how to make cheese like this. Now there are two more.

# Stoney Cross

## Made by Mike and Judy Smales and their team in Wiltshire

PASTEURISED COW'S MILK, VEGETARIAN RENNET

Stoney Cross has a gunmetal grey rind with a dusting of white *Penicillium* much like a traditional Caerphilly. The stoney aroma has just a light trace of mustiness, not so much a cellar as the inside of a country church on a day in early spring. The elastic texture of the paste breaks down in the mouth to deliver a delicate yet complex set of flavours. A zesty opening develops into butter and sweet milk with an earthy undertone and finishes with a steely minerality.

To this geeky cheese historian, the name suggested an allusion to the cheese cross that once indicated Salisbury's medieval cheese market, but on doing some actual research (that is, talking to Mike), it turns out to be a reference to the nearby First World War airfield.

Stoney Cross is an example of how, in cheesemaking, small changes can lead to big differences. The recipe is essentially the same as for the Smales' Old Winchester, but the curd is put into a different-shaped mould and matured in a high moisture environment, an elegant solution to the need for product diversification. As Mike says, 'Don't make your life any more complicated than necessary'.

# Suffolk Gold

## Made by Katharine and Jason Salisbury in Suffolk

PASTEURISED COW'S MILK, VEGETARIAN RENNET

'Suffolk Gold' sounds vastly more appetising than 'Suffolk Whang', 'Bang' or 'Thump', all names for the county's seventeenth-century skimmed milk cheese, which was reputed to be so hard and tasteless that even the rough Jack Tars of the Royal Navy refused to eat it. The poor quality of the old cheese was the fault of the cheesemongers of the time who forced the Suffolk producers to skim all the cream off their milk to make lucrative butter for the London market, and not at all to do with the *terroir* of Suffolk, which (as the Salisburys prove) can make lovely complex cheese. The 'gold' in the name refers to the rich colour of the paste which I'm sure owes something to the rich Suffolk pasture but is also down to their herd of Guernsey and Jersey cows and the excellent milk that they produce.

With its grey velvety mould rind, Suffolk Gold looks a lot like an Alpine Tomme, but is firmer and sharper. The cheese has a comforting aroma of old churches and butter with a bracing ammoniac tang, and a bright yoghurty sourness cuts through the rich creamy flavour from that good milk. You'll need to hurry if you want to try some, as the couple are about to move to the tiny island of Sark to run the island's dairy farm and hopefully carry on making smashing cheese.

# Thelma's Caerffili

## Made by the Adams family in Carmarthenshire

PASTEURISED COW'S MILK, VEGETARIAN RENNET

Thelma's Caerffili has quite a different appearance to its West Country cousins, made on the other side of the Severn Estuary. A light dusting of white mould overlays a cream-coloured rind, underneath which is a narrow strip of relatively firm breakdown. The paste has a firm moist crumble, and a bright fresh acidity rounding out into a milky caramelised flavour like a Caramac, the caramel bar of my 1970s childhood. The finish has a decent length for a young fresh cheese and shows a comforting homely note of condensed milk.

The cheese's name is the Welsh spelling of 'Caerphilly' and 'Thelma's' distinguishes this one from their younger Caerphilly. A picture of Thelma, resplendently attired in Egyptian headdress and reclining defiantly in a bathtub full of milk, appears on the packaging of this cheese. This Boudiccan pose was a protest agains the UK government's imposition of EU milk quotas that made the sale of liquid milk less profitable and was the motivation for the Adams family moving into cheesemaking.

# Ticklemore

## Made by Debbie Mumford and her team in Devon

 PASTEURISED GOAT'S MILK, VEGETARIAN RENNET

In its appearance alone, Ticklemore is one of the more intriguing cheeses – it looks like a fluffy white flying saucer. Goat's cheeses tend to be smaller than cow's milk cheeses, partly because you don't get as much milk from a goat. Ticklemore's larger size and firmer texture make it stand out, and the larger mass means that the softening effect of the rind is reduced. Under the snowy rind there is a slim creamy layer of breakdown, but the main body retains a moist chalky texture and a gentle zesty flavour with just a piquant hint of goatiness which adds complexity.

For this reason I often suggest Ticklemore to anyone who has been put off goat's milk cheese by a more animalistic example. The light open texture and fresh flavour also make this the perfect cheese for a summer picnic, perhaps with a green salad and a cool glass of some crispy white wine. Robin Congdon, who developed the cheese in the 1970s, generously handed over the recipe to Debbie and Mark, who make it on the Sharpham Estate, home of some rather smashing crispy whites. See where I'm going with this?

# Wiltshire Loaf

## Made by Ceri Cryer in Wiltshire

PASTEURISED COW'S MILK, VEGETARIAN RENNET

The paste of Wiltshire Loaf is a pale yellow, deepening toward the rind, and has a scattering of small holes. The texture is light and open, less dense than Cheddar but not as crumbly as Caerphilly, and the flavour is milky with a touch of sweetness, green herb notes, tied together with a gentle citrusy acidity and a light cream and mineral finish.

Wiltshire Loaf is a territorial cheese and shares the typical characteristics of that uniquely British family, with its light texture, bright acidity and mineral notes. While all territorials suffered greatly from the increase of factory cheesemaking and the rise of supermarkets after the Second World War, Wiltshire Loaf's decline began earlier and was more complete. From the 1870s, competition with cheap American imports and the growth of the urban liquid milk market decimated farmhouse cheesemaking, until by 1914 it was all but extinct in the county. Ceri is the fifth generation of her family to make cheese on their farm, and it makes me enormously happy that in 2005 she decided to revive this once lost cheese and bring it back to the national cheeseboard.

# Yorkshire Pecorino

## Made by Mario Olianas in North Yorkshire

🐑 PASTEURISED SHEEP'S MILK, ANIMAL RENNET

If you have only had Pecorino outside Italy, you might be more familiar with aged hard cheeses like Pecorino Sardo or Romano. Younger and softer styles like Pecorino *fresco* and *semi-stagionato* don't tend to travel so much. This thirty-day-old Yorkshire version, based on a Pecorino *fresco*, might then be a bit of a revelation.

It's a lovely example of cross-cultural fertilisation, and has the broadest *terroir* of any cheese I know – the starter culture is from Sardinia and the milk from just outside Harrogate. The rind has a light dusting of blue and white moulds that add complexity, and the supple paste is ivory with a scattering of small holes. In its aroma I get sheep, a little ammonia and a hint of cool stone.

The flavour is complex, perfectly balanced and evocative, a slight acidity, gentle salt and then a note of freshly cut wood, cedary, resinous, and at once I find myself transported to an austere yet beautiful Mediterranean setting, where among scrub and exposed stone hardy sheep graze on thorny bushes and straggling rosemary.

# Hard cheeses

# Hard cheeses

Allerdale . . . . . . . . . . . . . . . 164
Anster . . . . . . . . . . . . . . . . 165
Appleby's Cheshire . . . . . . . 166
Berkswell . . . . . . . . . . . . . 167
Bermondsey Hard Pressed . 168
Cais Na Tire . . . . . . . . . . . . 169
Cerwyn Mature . . . . . . . . . 170
Clonmore . . . . . . . . . . . . . . 171
Coolattin . . . . . . . . . . . . . 172
Coolea . . . . . . . . . . . . . . . 173
Corra Linn . . . . . . . . . . . . . 174
Crump's Double
Gloucester . . . . . . . . . . . . . 175
Cumberland Farmhouse . . 176
Derg Cheddar . . . . . . . . . . . 177
Doddington . . . . . . . . . . . . 178
Drumlin . . . . . . . . . . . . . . . 179
Dunlop . . . . . . . . . . . . . . . 180
Fifteen Fields . . . . . . . . . . . 181
Goatisan . . . . . . . . . . . . . . 182
Hafod . . . . . . . . . . . . . . . . 183
Hardy's . . . . . . . . . . . . . . . 184
Hegarty's Cheddar . . . . . . . 185
Isle of Mull Cheddar . . . . . 186
Keen's Cheddar . . . . . . . . . 187
Killeen . . . . . . . . . . . . . . . 188
Kirkham's Lancashire . . . . . 189
Kit Calvert Wensleydale . . . 190
Lincolnshire Poacher . . . . . 191
Little Hereford . . . . . . . . . . 192
Loch Arthur . . . . . . . . . . . 193
Lord of the Hundreds . . . . . 194
Martell's Double
Gloucester . . . . . . . . . . . . . 195
Mayfield . . . . . . . . . . . . . . 196
Montgomery's Cheddar . . . 197
Mossfield . . . . . . . . . . . . . 198
Norfolk Dapple . . . . . . . . . 199
Old Winchester . . . . . . . . . 200
Owd Ewe . . . . . . . . . . . . . 201
Pitchfork Cheddar . . . . . . . 202
Quicke's Cheddar . . . . . . . . 203
St Andrews . . . . . . . . . . . . 204
Saint Gall . . . . . . . . . . . . . 205
Shropshire . . . . . . . . . . . . . 206
Sparkenhoe Red Leicester . 207
Spenwood . . . . . . . . . . . . . 208
Summerfield . . . . . . . . . . . 209
Teifi . . . . . . . . . . . . . . . . . 210
Templegall . . . . . . . . . . . . 211
Tinto . . . . . . . . . . . . . . . . 212
Wells Alpine . . . . . . . . . . . 213
Westcombe Cheddar . . . . . 214

# Hard cheeses

Hard cheeses have more moisture removed during their making and maturing than other varieties. The lower moisture and hard texture mean that these cheeses keep longer, are more durable and are a more concentrated source of nutrition. Longer-keeping cheese has, historically, been at an advantage if your making season was short, because you could make plenty of cheese in the spring and summer to keep you going in the long barren winter. More robust cheeses are also better able to survive a journey to markets, which is a boon for cheesemakers in more remote locations like the Alps, or indeed deepest Somerset. And, as a concentrated form of nutrition, hard cheese has been an excellent addition to the ration packs of soldiers and other travellers. Hittite records from the second millennium BCE mention aged soldiers' cheese, a reference to its hardness rather than suitability for elderly veterans.

These were historical reasons to make hard cheese, and with modern farming methods, food technology and transport they are no longer as pressing. But there is another benefit to longer-keeping cheese, in that it creates deeper and more complex flavours, which, given that few of us these days are setting off to find the Northwest Passage, is of more pressing interest.

For anyone from British Isles, Cheddar is the first hard cheese that springs to mind, so let us have a look at how it is made.

The first step is to acidify and set the milk using starter culture and rennet. The set curd, at this stage a fragile gel, is then cut into cubes with a pair of many-bladed knives. After a brief rest, known as *healing*, the curd, still sitting in the whey, is heated, a step that in British cheesemaking is termed the *scald*. For Cheddar the scald temperature is around 38°C, although I suspect if I got ten Cheddar makers around a vat there would be ten different opinions on this. Throughout the heating step, the curd must be stirred to stop it clumping together into masses that would heat unevenly, a task that to the great relief of modern cheesemakers is now mechanised and carried out by a couple of giant egg beaters that whirl around the vat.

After sufficient scalding, the stirring stops and the curd is allowed to matt together into a single mass, which sinks to the bottom of the vat – a step known as *pitching*, or *whey off* – and a valve is opened and the whey allowed to drain off. To assist this the cheesemakers pull the curd to the sides of the vat, creating a channel. At this point the curd is firm and rubbery, so firm that it can be cut into blocks (about the size of breeze blocks). These are stacked around the side of the vat, and then re-stacked so that the block on the bottom goes to the top, squeezing more moisture from the blocks and causing the curd to knit together, which results in a more dense cheese. This process appears to be unique to British cheesemaking and, although Cheddar is not the only British cheese that employs this step, it is known as *cheddaring*.

Once enough cheddaring has gone on, the cheesemakers use their remaining energy to feed the blocks through a mill, a sort of mangle with teeth, breaking the curd up once again into a mass of small particles into which handfuls of salt are chucked and mixed through. The milled and salted curd is then shovelled into moulds, which these days look like gigantic aluminium stock pots, and put into presses for the night, no doubt to the considerable relief of the cheesemakers.

The next day the cheeses are knocked out of their moulds, bound in cloth and then rubbed (in lard, if you are in the West Country). The cloth-plus-fat combination makes an optimal covering, allowing enough evaporation to create a firm texture but not allowing the cheeses to dry out. It also allows some mould penetration, which adds musty and earthy notes to the complex palette of flavours in a traditional Cheddar.

After binding, larding and some more time in the press, the cheeses are laid down in barns – or, in the case of Westcombe Cheddar, a gigantic cave dug into the side of a hill. They will mature in a cool moist atmosphere for anything from twelve months to two years. These twenty-four-kilo cheeses need to be turned regularly as they mature, so that their bottoms don't get sticky, and evaporation and mould penetration proceed equally on all side of the cheese. With thousands of cheeses in store, this is a task that would make Hercules quail, although nowadays there are cheese-turning robots to do the job.

What makes Cheddar Cheddar is technique more than *terroir*. Excellent Cheddars are made throughout Britain and Ireland including the Welsh Hafod, Irish Coolattin and St Andrews from the east coast of Scotland. In fact you can make cheese anywhere in the world and call it Cheddar. West Country cheesemakers have long made attempts to establish some sort of protection and valorisation of Cheddar from its original home and in 1994 registered *West Country Farmhouse Cheddar* as a PDO (Protected Domain of Origin) with the European Union. This cheese can only be made in the counties of Dorset, Somerset, Devon and Cornwall, and the specification also includes certain techniques that must be carried out in order to call the cheese Cheddar. This PDO allows raw or pasteurised milk, and animal or vegetarian rennet, to be used and includes both traditional cloth-bound and plastic-wrapped block cheese. Cheesemakers and mongers argue about whether block, vegetarian rennet or pasteurised cheeses should be called Farmhouse Cheddar until the cows come home, a phrase that for once in this case is literally true.

Montgomery's, Keen's, Westcombe and Pitchfork Cheddars comprise a more exclusive group called *Artisan Somerset Cheddar*. Registered with Slow Food in 2003, this group of cheeses is called a presidium, a similar sort of thing to a PDO without the same level of legal heft. As the name signals, the *terroir* has been reduced to a single county and the presidium also stipulates that cheese can only be made with milk from the maker's own farm, the milk must be raw, the rennet animal, the cheese cloth-bound and aged for at least eleven months.

Of course, there are plenty of other hard cheeses in Britain and Ireland. The traditional ones are all members of a group unique to Britain called the territorials. There are different ways of defining this group, and I can see the merits to all of them, but my preferred definition, and one which suits the purpose of this book, is that they are produced from cow's milk and are mostly hard (although Wensleydale, comes in hard and semi-soft versions), often crumbly, quite mild, fairly acidic, and tend to be cloth-bound. Within those terms the territorials are Caerphilly, Cheshire, Double and Single Gloucester, Dunlop, Lancashire, Leicester, Wensleydale and Wiltshire Loaf (which we met in the previous – semi-soft – chapter).

Even within this family, each style has specific techniques that make it unique. For traditional Farmhouse Lancashire, some of the curd from each day of making is set aside to 'mellow', so that it softens and develops flavour. The mellowed curd from a couple of previous days is mixed with younger firmer curd before being put into moulds, contributing to a moist and open texture that Lancashire maker Graham Kirkham describes deliciously as 'butter crumble'. Traditional Cheshire makers use a relatively large amount of starter culture so that, in the initial stages of the make, the acidity increase results in a more crumbly texture and a bright fresh acidity. For Double Gloucester the curd is scalded to about the same temperature as Cheddar, but the curd is not cheddared but just cut and turned, resulting in a creamier and firmer texture than Cheshire but one less dense than Cheddar.

Since the Cheese Renaissance of the 1970s, in which British and Irish makers borrowed from traditional continental methods, two other methods of hard cheesemaking have become popular. For Alpine cheeses, like Comté and Gruyère, and their counterparts on this side of the Channel like the Irish Templegall, the curd is cut into much smaller particles than for Cheddar or the territorials, and heated to a higher temperature – from 40°C to as much as 55°C – and, rather than being pitched, cheddared and milled, the curd is lifted out of the whey and put straight into the mould. These techniques and other factors result in the characteristic sweetness and elastic texture of cheeses in this style. Dutch cheeses like Gouda have inspired cheeses such as Doddington from Northumberland and the Irish Coolea to use a method called *washed-curd*, in which some whey is run off and hot water added. This creates a more dense elastic texture than traditional British styles, and also results in sweeter cheese. In one of those seeming paradoxes common to cheesemaking, by reducing the amount of lactose (sugar) at this stage, you actually end up with sweeter cheese, because there is less available to be converted into lactic acid during the make and maturation.

# Allerdale

## Made by Carolyn Fairbairn and her team in Cumbria

UNPASTEURISED GOAT'S MILK, ANIMAL RENNET

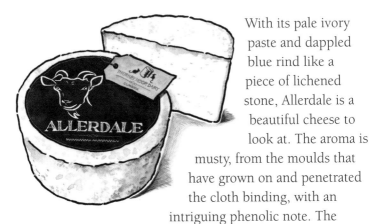

With its pale ivory paste and dappled blue rind like a piece of lichened stone, Allerdale is a beautiful cheese to look at. The aroma is musty, from the moulds that have grown on and penetrated the cloth binding, with an intriguing phenolic note. The texture, while firm, is giving and moist. At first it comes on clean, fresh and simple, but as that fudgey texture breaks down and warms in the mouth, a savoury flavour like cured meat develops, intertwined with floral notes and a developing acidity, with a long complex finish leaving an astringent tingle on the tongue.

You can barely sense the goatiness in this cheese which is a tribute to Carolyn's skill. Goat's milk is delicate and difficult to work with. As Carolyn's daughter Leonie says, rough and impatient handling can 'bruise' the milk, releasing more goatiness and making harder, drier cheese. Carolyn began making Allerdale, her first cheese, in 1979, making her one of the originals of the Cheese Renaissance. She is completely self-taught, and her cheeses, while loosely based on traditional smallholders' methods, are all her own. 'Like Mary Holbrook, in the north, without a farm,' says Leonie.

# Anster

## Made by Jane Stewart in Fife

UNPASTEURISED COW'S MILK, ANIMAL RENNET

Anster is a surprising cheese. Its ivory colour suggests sheep's milk rather than cow's, and the texture looks like a pale Lancashire. Actually, the aroma is more tart than buttery, and the texture more squeaky than the moist crumble of a Lancashire. The flavour comes on with a bracing sourness, develops some mustardy heat, and finishes with a note of savoury green herb like chives or wild garlic.

Anster is named for the nearby fishing village of Anstruther, and I wonder if the sea air and the moist salty pasture may have influenced the flavour and texture. Its recipe is based to an extent on northern English cheeses like Cheshire and Wensleydale, both of which are quite pale, which might account for its appearance. There is another characteristic, a certain milky freshness, present in Ansters made with a particular strain of starter culture, but you'll only taste this if you buy the cheese from the Courtyard Dairy in Lancashire, whose customers and owner found that they preferred that flavour profile. So *terroir*, method and market have combined to create this unique character, plus – of course – the skill and craft of its maker.

# Appleby's Cheshire

## Made by the Appleby family and Garry Gray in Shropshire

☙ UNPASTEURISED COW'S MILK, ANIMAL RENNET

You can tell where someone is from by what colour they think Cheshire is. For the Londoners, it is an enticing sunset pink; for the people of Chester and its environs, an austere china white. This divide goes back a long way. In its natural state Cheshire is a pure white colour, the result of acidity leaching carotene out of the curd. While this has no effect on the cheese's succulence, seventeenth-century London cheesemongers feared it would put their customers off and asked the cheesemakers to dye cheese for the southern market. The distinction persists today and the Applebys dye some of their cheese – with the flavourless vegetable dye annatto – and leave some as nature intended.

If it's bothering you that this Cheshire is from Shropshire, relax. It's just that the style became so successful in the seventeenth century that farmers from adjacent counties in England and Wales wanted in on the act. Cheese knows no borders. Appleby's happens to be my favourite Cheshire. Made with raw milk from the family's herd and cloth-bound, its moist crumbly texture and delicate minerality are pure delight. I could eat a ton of it.

# Berkswell

## Made by the Fletcher family in Warwickshire

UNPASTEURISED SHEEP'S MILK, ANIMAL RENNET

The colour of wet straw with a pebbly rind and domed shape, Berkswell looks like an ancient petrified bee skep, indicating an exciting maturity. Young Berkswells can show a note of pineapple so pronounced that opening a cheese can be like cutting into a fresh fruit. Older cheeses have more of a sheepy lanolin note with an edge of ammonia, still laced with that tropical tang. The flavours open with an ammoniac bite, developing into cooked sweetness appropriate to the firm fudge texture of the paste. Savoury caramelised lamb and a hint of rosewater intertwine,  finishing on a gentle but insistent astringency. Together this creates the effect of a lamb tagine with the classic Moroccan mix of rosewater, meat and spices.

The Fletchers began sheep dairying in 1989 when the UK government's somewhat un-nuanced application of EU milk quotas made cattle uneconomic. As with so many farmers in that period, any memory of cheesemaking in the family had been lost. That is, until under a coat of paint on an old door were found the words 'Cheese Room', the floorboards of which had been smoothed and worn by the whey dripping from the young cheeses over generations of cheesemaking.

# Bermondsey Hard Pressed

## Made by Bill Oglethorpe and his team in London

🐄 UNPASTEURISED COW'S MILK, ANIMAL RENNET

Bill Oglethorpe, who comes from Zambian farming stock by way of a Swiss agricultural college, is one of my favourite cheesemakers, and one of my favourite people in the world. He is living proof of my theory that to make great cheese it helps to be a throughly decent human being – and a little eccentric too. We worked together in the cellars at Neal's Yard Dairy, where he taught me everything I know about looking after cheese, which in a sense is nothing, in that seeking certainty about any aspect of cheese or its production is a fool's errand. This attitude is exemplified in one of my favourite Sayings of Bill: 'If you don't play with your cheese, it'll play with you.'

Bill's Bermondsey Hard Pressed – the name alludes to the harsh economics of cheesemaking – has a dense elastic paste, and a varying panoply of flavours that can include sweetness, spiciness, white chocolate, browned beef and just a hint of the barnyard. Inspired by Alpine cheeses like Gruyère or Appenzeller, it's made in a traditional copper vat in a railway arch in Bermondsey. So that's a Zambian making a Swiss cheese in London. See what I mean?

# Cais Na Tire

## Made by Barry and Lorraine Cahalan in County Tipperary

PASTEURISED SHEEP'S MILK, ANIMAL RENNET

Cais Na Tire has a warm yellow colour, unusual for a sheep's milk cheese, and the aroma is novel – buttered popcorn, no less. The flavour is toasty, too, with notes of caramelised sugar, and the texture, instead of the dry flakiness of an aged Pecorino or Manchego, has retained some moisture and melts luxuriously in the mouth.

Barry and Lorraine Cahalan did not come upon cheese-making accidentally from a background in, say, engineering or philosophy like other contemporary cheesemakers I know. Both from farming backgrounds, they met at school, went on to agricultural college and set up a dairy farm on family land. Their story also displays that pragmatism typical to farmers and cheesemakers. Farming cattle was beyond their means and so they decided to go with sheep. As to how they learned cheesemaking and developed the recipe for their cheese, they are firmly back in the context of contemporary cheesemaking, with its cross-cultural influences and life choices. They owe both craft and recipe to neighbouring cheesemaker, Marion Roeleveld, a Dutchwoman who left a career in journalism to move to Ireland and make cheese.

# Cerwyn Mature

## Made by the Jennings family in Pembrokeshire

🐄 PASTEURISED COW'S MILK, VEGETARIAN RENNET

Showing a rugged individuality, Cerwyn is very much its own thing rather than an established style like Cheddar. The paste is pale for a cow's milk cheese, and the texture is firm and dense. The rind has a slight orange tinge like a washed-rind but the cheese has a very gentle aroma with only the merest trace of funk. The flavour is sweet and astringent with a grapey note that I recognise from a Munster, and a hot peppery finish. All together, the flavours are pretty intense, surprisingly so for a cheese with such a mild aroma. Honouring what seems to me a singularly Celtic and ancient habit, Cerwyn is named for a mountain, Foel Cwmcerwyn, the highest peak in the Preseli Hills, whose view through the cheese-room window inspires the cheesemakers as they work.

This view must have been quite a change for David and Cynthia Jennings, who in 1983 had just returned to the verdant county of Pembrokeshire from the Middle East, where they had been helping to set up dairies in Libya and Yemen. If the Jennings are as rugged and individualistic as their cheese, they are just as adventurous and generous of spirit.

# Clonmore

## Made by Tom and Lena Biggane in County Cork

PASTEURISED GOAT'S MILK, VEGETARIAN RENNET

The paste of a Clonmore is an unexpectedly dark shade for a goat's cheese – more vellum than snowy white – and that is not the only out-of-the-ordinary aspect of this truly fascinating cheese. The animalistic aroma is enlivened by a marvellously surprising note of roasted peanuts. The paste is dotted with small holes suggesting the work of propionic bacteria that give sweet and nutty flavours and are common in Gouda-style cheese – of which this is an example.

This is a salty cheese, but that seems to work well with a flavour profile that comprises sweetness, a floral note and a goaty presence I could only just sense, so well are the flavours intertwined.

As is common in goat dairying, Tom and Lena Biggane allow their goats to follow the natural lactation cycle and so only make cheese from March to November, which makes for happy healthy animals and really great cheese. Another thing that contributes to great cheese is good land, and Tom and Lena's farm is in an area called the Golden Vale, which covers parts of Limerick, Tipperary and Cork and is considered to be Ireland's, if not the world's, finest pasture.

# Coolattin

## Made by Tom Burgess in County Carlow

UNPASTEURISED COW'S MILK, ANIMAL RENNET

I know you shouldn't judge a book by its cover or a cheese by its binding, but the strikingly beautiful crimson cloth that covers a Coolattin really does draw you to it. Happily, what's underneath lives up to this promise. On the nose I get caramelised onions and a hint of fermented fruits, like blowsy apples on an orchard floor. The texture is firmly chewy and delivers a gentle clean flavour, but as the cheese breaks down in the mouth this builds quickly to a warm farminess and exciting acidity. In the finish is a volatile sweetness like a hint of pear drops and a spicy astringent feeling persists on the tongue for a while afterwards.

Tom Burgess only makes cheese when his cows are out on pasture, and only uses milk from the morning milking. He points out that the morning milk is absolutely fresh and goes straight into the vat – 'Pasture to Cheddar the same day', is how he puts it. Most farmhouse Cheddars are aged to around twelve to eighteen months, but Tom ages his to a full two years, conferring complexity and bite. As to the richness of the texture, we have the rich high fat milk of his happy Jersey cross cows to thank for that.

# Coolea

## Made by Dickie Willems in County Cork

🐾 PASTEURISED COW'S MILK, ANIMAL RENNET

I might have said that other cheeses in this collection are sweet. I may have even bandied about the word 'caramel'. All these things are true and I stand by them. Then we come to Coolea. Its rich sunset yellow colour holds the promise of sweet treats to come: the dense, chewy texture sits somewhere between toffee and fudge, and the flavour – burnt sugar, roasted hazelnuts, salt and just a hint of umami – is like an incredibly sophisticated salted caramel. And, just in case you thought your cheese eating experience couldn't get any more outlandish, you should also know that this cheese pairs well with chilli jam.

Maybe cheeses, like pets, take on the character of their owners/makers. The Willems family moved to Ireland from their native Holland in the 1970s. Their son Dickie, who makes the cheese these days, speaks with a Dutch-Irish accent, and so does his cheese: Coolea is based on a Dutch Gouda and derives its sumptuous richness from the ambrosial pastures of County Cork. The cheese I have been describing is sold at around a year. The extra mature, at around five years old, is something else. Crystalline, tingling, a slight bitterness intertwined with residual sugar, Coolea is a cheese to build a dream on.

# Corra Linn

## Made by Angela Cairns and the Erringtons in Lanarkshire

🐑 UNPASTEURISED SHEEP'S MILK, ANIMAL RENNET

Like many of the Erringtons' cheeses, Corra Linn is named
for a geographical feature, in this case a waterfall on the Clyde
River, immortalised in a poem by Wordsworth and painted by
Turner. That's quite something to live up to for a cheese, but
I reckon Corra's done okay. A guest at one of my tastings said
'fairgrounds' on smelling this cheese. Teasing that apart, I'd say
that candy floss, popcorn and straw feature in the aroma. The
paste has a moist fudgey texture and notes of honeycomb and
caramel, with only a hint of sheepiness and a light presence of
salt to remind you that you are eating a savoury product.

Cheesemakers often have very practical reasons for developing a new cheese, and Corra Linn is no exception. Sheep
tend to give milk only in the spring
and summer, and the Erringtons
were finding that, if they made
enough of their signature Lanark
Blue to sell all year round, the
older batches got too fierce
for all but the most jaded
palates. The solution was
to make a hard cheese that
would mature more slowly
and retain a more gentle
flavour, and Corra Linn was
born. Rarely has such a lovely
thing come forth from mere
product diversification.

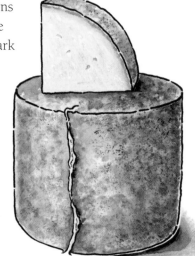

# Crump's Double Gloucester

## Made by Jonathan Crump in Gloucester

 UNPASTEURISED COW'S MILK, VEGETARIAN RENNET

The dimpled rind of this cheese has a light scattering of blue-grey moulds with a lovely orange glow coming through – traditionally Double Gloucester is coloured with the vegetable dye, annatto. There is a gentle musty aroma from the rind and a malted milk note from the sunny orange paste. The cheese has a soft fudge texture and an upfront acidity which  builds into a fizzy tang and a long finish. Butter, earth and flinty minerality combine with spritzy acidity to create a mouthwatering juicy effect.

Double Gloucester achieved renown at home and abroad in the eighteenth century, even challenging the dominance of its more delicate cousin, Cheshire. The most highly prized cheeses came from the Vale of Berkeley, where Jonathan farms, so he was already onto a winner with *terroir* and breed – Gloucesters are known for the quality of their milk. Of course, you still need plenty of skill and commitment to make consistently good cheese, especially from raw milk, which can change so much from day to day. I asked Jonathan if he found raw milk cheesemaking particularly challenging, to which he replied with an offhand humility typical of cheesemakers, 'I don't know. I've never done it any other way.'

# Cumberland Farmhouse

## Made by Carolyn Fairbairn and her team in Cumbria

UNPASTEURISED COW'S MILK, ANIMAL RENNET

Cumberland Farmhouse has a lovely green and buttery aroma, like buttercups in a summer meadow. The flavour is mild but complex, as you would expect from a British cloth-bound cheese with more than a hint of the territorial about it. Opening with a buttery flavour cut through with tangy acidity, mustard then appears, followed appropriately by musty, umami and sweet notes that taken together taste like a cured sausage of the salami variety. The texture is so soft that a knife dragged lightly across the cut surface will pick up cheese and spread it like butter. This is luxuriant cheese.

When Carolyn Fairbairn set out making cheese in 1979 she tried to find records of a traditional Cumbrian cheese to revive, sadly in vain. The county is more famous for its butter. However, like her Allerdale Cumberland, her Farmhouse is based on old smallholders' recipes for cheese, and is made from the milk of a local herd of Shorthorns. A breed famed for their kind temperament and the quality of their milk, they were Britain's traditional cheesemaking cow. Also, Carolyn's daughter Leonie told me that Carolyn wanted to make a cheese for Cumbria, that the county should have its own territorial, which it now does.

# Derg Cheddar

## Made by Paddy and Kay Cooney in County Tipperary

 UNPASTEURISED COW'S MILK, ANIMAL RENNET

The Irish have been keen cheesemakers since the Neolithic period but, tragically, indigenous cheese styles disappeared during the British occupation. In the nineteenth century, Irish cheesemakers began copying English styles like Cheddar, so successfully that they managed to take a considerable slice of the British market for their cheese. What I find even more pleasing is that the Irish versions have their own definite unique character, which must come from Irish farming culture as much as geographical *terroir*.

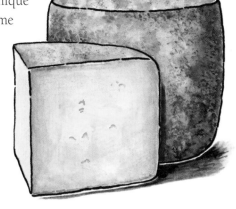

Derg has the rich sunset yellow I am used to in a West Country Cheddar, but in other aspects it is very much its own creature. There is a spread of small holes throughout the paste that suggest the work of propionic bacteria, a family responsible for the holes and sweet nutty flavours in Dutch and Alpine cheese. The texture is firm but more elastic than crumbly and I get an appetising aroma of leeks and butter. There is also a Gouda-like sweetness in the flavour, that may come in part from those propionic bacteria, and a gently tingling acidity. I also get a buttery flavour, and up against the rind the cheese has a dark earthy note.

# Doddington

## Made by Maggie Maxwell in Northumberland

🐾 UNPASTEURISED COW'S MILK, ANIMAL RENNET

Doddington, in Maggie Maxwell's own words, 'lies somewhere between a Leicester and a Cheddar' and its texture bears this out, with some of the softer chewiness of the former and a bit of the dense friability of the latter. Its beefy savouriness – another Cheddar-like quality – is tempered with a sweet flavour much like a Dutch cheese. Maggie studied cheesemaking in Holland and wheels of Doddington, with their rounded edges and red wax coats, not only look like Dutch cheeses but have some of the sweetness of a Gouda. I find this sweetness quite different from the burnt sugar flavour in that other Gouda-like cheese, Coolea. It's cleaner and sharper, which is perhaps an effect of the higher acidity interacting with that sweetness.

Maggie's family were originally from Scotland – her mother's side from Ayrshire, where they made Dunlop cheese. When her mother's family moved to Northumberland, they milked their cows in the morning at Kilmarnock, loaded them on a train, and at the end of the day walked them up the hill to the new farm at Thornington in the foothills of the Cheviots to milk them in the evening.

# Drumlin

## Made by Silke and Tom Cropp in County Cavan

UNPASTEURISED COW'S MILK, VEGETARIAN RENNET

Drumlins, little three-inch-high cylinders, come in a brown paper wrapping tied up with string, which looks so lovely, and is such fun to unwrap that I almost think all cheeses should come like that. Under the wrapping, the cheese has a rumpled look from its draining cloth and the rind is the light fawn of an artist's canvas. The paste is a warm yellow, shading to a richer sunset inside the rind, showing its ripening action on the cheese. The aroma has notes of warm hay and butter and the flavour makes me think of a salty intense Wensleydale, with a little more umami. The edible rind adds a musty note and there is a long pleasant finish of green herbs.

I would eat a ton of this on a cheeseboard, and I can tell you from experience that with a dollop of chutney it makes a great sandwich.

A Drumlin, from the Irish *droimnín*, meaning 'littlest ridge', is a glacial hill in the shape of a half-buried egg, and the name references the drumlin pastures on which the animals graze. It's a fitting choice for a cheese that looks like the artefact of an ancient geological process.

# Dunlop

### Made by Ann Dorward in Ayrshire

PASTEURISED COW'S MILK, VEGETARIAN RENNET

You sometimes see this style advertised as 'Dunlop Cheddar', which is a shame, as this is a distinct variety, native to Scotland, and ought to be celebrated as such. Ann Dorward's Dunlop is certainly worth doing so. Under its cloth binding, the rind has a lovely dappled orange brown colour. The paste is a rich, warm yellow and smells of buttered popcorn. There's a definite fudginess to the texture and the flavour is sweet and buttery with just the mildest hint of cow. I would have said this is quite a delicate cheese overall, but, while the flavour comes on sweet and mild, the acidity becomes more and more pronounced, finishing on a sharp bite.

Although that acidity is reminiscent of a heftier Cheddar, Dunlop is very much a thing in itself. In fact, when this cheese first appeared, its distinctive quality got its maker into trouble. Barbara Gilmour, an Ayrshire cheesemaker, started making the cheese in the seventeenth century from full-cream Ayrshire milk. Locals who had only eaten hard dry skimmed milk cheese before couldn't believe cheese could be this good without supernatural intervention, and accused Gilmour of witchcraft. Thankfully she beat the rap and carried on making cheese.

# Fifteen Fields

## Made by Eamonn Lonergan in County Waterford and matured by Mark Brooker at Sheridans

UNPASTEURISED COW'S MILK, VEGETARIAN RENNET

The Lonergans have been farming in the Waterford parish of Knockanore for more than sixty years. They began cheesemaking in 1987 with the Irish Cheese Renaissance in full flower. The name Knockanore, meaning 'hill of gold', refers to an ancient treasure – the lush pasture of the rolling hills around their farm.

This cheese is named for the fifteen fields on which their pedigree Friesians graze, and is made only between May and October, when the cows are out on pasture. It's then expertly matured at Sheridans Cheesemonger's warehouse by Mark Brooker. The paste is an ivory colour rather than the deeper yellow more common in cow's milk cheese. I can taste sweetness, all that lovely grass and a caramel note, and the cheese has a rambunctious intensity that reminds me more of French Cantal than classic Cheddar. The finish is long and astringent, leaving a sharp sensation on my tongue. The cheeses are not bound in cloth, and this is where Mark's work adds character to the cheese. Kept in humid conditions, they are washed in lightly salted water, encouraging the growth of moulds and yeasts that add complexity to the flavour.

# Goatisan

## Made by Iona Hill in Yorkshire

🐐 PASTEURISED GOAT'S MILK, VEGETARIAN RENNET

Goatisan was the first of Iona Hill's natural rinded cheeses, based on her wax-covered Original Goat. She told me that the main challenge had been to get the balance of moisture right in the recipe, so that the cheese can mature without the wax and yet retain moisture. Hard goat's cheeses can be very dry. This one gives only a little when squeezed, yet leaves a trace of moisture on the fingertips, such that I think Iona got that balance just right. Aged vegetarian rennet cheeses often tend to bitterness, and this is not so with Goatisan. Iona says that the crucial point is not to leave the curd to coagulate for too long before cutting, but as to what 'too long' means you'll have to make your own cheese to figure that out.

Goatisan's paste is a lovely pale ivory, and the texture, as promised, is hard yet moist. The aroma shows a trace of fresh green herbs; the firm texture, breaking down in the mouth, melts away rather than coating the palate and, in combination with a citrus note in the flavour makes me think of a syllabub or some other eighteenth-century dairy-based dessert. The overall delicacy and simplicity of the flavour lift in the finish with a light astringent tingle.

# Hafod

## Made by the Holden family and their team in Ceredigion

PASTEURISED COW'S MILK, ANIMAL RENNET

'Low and slow' is how Hafod is made. The lower temperature leads to slower acidification of the curd, and this in turn means that the cheese retains more moisture. Unlike the more boisterous Keen's Cheddar, Hafod has a relatively gentle acidity along with a buttery note and something slightly toasty. This may be the result of that slow acidification, and also that the cows that give their milk for this mellow yet complex cheese are Ayrshires, whose milk is richer in butterfat than the more common Friesian-Holsteins.

Hafod is so soft compared to many contemporary varieties that one Somerset cheese fancier I met refused to believe it was Cheddar, claiming an authority rooted in their county of origin. Funnily enough, as the recipe is based on a turn-of-the-century method developed by acclaimed cheesemaker Dora Saker, Hafod, even though Welsh in its origin, has as good a claim as any to Cheddar authenticity.

Made on Bwlchwernen Fawr, a farm in West Wales, Hafod is named for the summer lodge that the men would stay in when they took the cattle up for their seasonal grazing on the lush pastures high in the hills. Its name should be said as if sung by a Welsh tenor.

# Hardy's

## Made by Peter Morgan in Dorset

🐑 PASTEURISED SHEEP'S MILK, VEGETARIAN RENNET

Hardy's is rubbed in rapeseed oil and then allowed to develop a natural mould rind, a traditional Spanish practice for hard sheep's cheeses like Manchego. The folds and gathers of the draining cloths have left their mark on the rind, which, with its sheen and dark brown colour, looks like the ancient leather binding of a medieval grimoire. The aroma is mildly sheepy with a caramel note and the paste has that perfect balance of hardness and moist fudginess. The flavour is milky with caramel notes developing into dark chocolate, with fresh hay and an astringent tingle in the finish.

Hardy's is, of course, a fine name for a Dorset cheese, and a read of *Tess of the D'Urbervilles*, set in his beloved West Country, has plenty of detail to satisfy the literary cheesemonger, including milkmaids singing to the cows to encourage them to let down their milk, a seduction that takes place over a cheese vat, and a lovely passage in which Tess is lulled to sleep in the dairymaids' dormitory above the milk room by 'the smell of the cheeses in the adjoining cheese-loft, and the measured dripping of the whey from the wrings (cheese-presses) downstairs'.

# Hegarty's Cheddar

## Made by Dan Hegarty and Jean-Baptiste Enjelvin in Co. Cork

PASTEURISED COW'S MILK, VEGETARIAN RENNET

Hegarty's is pale for a Cheddar, and the aroma is reminiscent of happy cows in a nice warm barn on fresh straw. Perhaps there's a word for that in Gaelic. The texture is quite soft, though still firmer than a nineteenth-century style like Hafod. While the acidity is quite restrained, there is an exciting astringency to the flavour, some earthiness and a caramel finish quite distinct from other Cheddars. In fact, like other Irish examples, Hegarty's has a unique character that sets it apart from English Cheddar.

The Hegartys have been farming their land, just outside Cork City, for five generations, but only began cheesemaking in 2001, when sons Dan and John came back from their studies and realised they were going to need to find a new income stream if the farm was to support both of them. The boys built the cheese room themselves and made their first batch. They then had to wait twelve months until the cheese matured and they would know if the new business venture had a future – a problem for all new Cheddar makers. Happily the cheese was okay, although it apparently took another four years to really nail it – an impressively steep learning curve in the world of cheese.

# Isle of Mull Cheddar

## Made by the Reade family on the Isle of Mull

 UNPASTEURISED COW'S MILK, ANIMAL RENNET

Cow's milk cheeses are usually a deep yellow, Cheddar particularly so. Isle of Mull is a pale ivory, more like a sheep's milk, except that sheep don't tend to produce great big twenty-four-kilo cheeses. The distinctive colour and the flavour of this Cheddar are a perfect example of *terroir* and its effect on cheese. The Reade family came up from Somerset to farm on the Isle of Mull in 1979.

Given their origin, it's no surprise that they decided to make Cheddar, but the land had its own contribution to make to the character of their cheese. Summers are brief this far north, and the grass is in shorter supply, so the Reades enrich their herd's diet with draff, the spent barley mash from the Isle's whisky distillery at Tobermory.

While the pale colour of the cheese might be down to the lower proportion of grass, as if in compensation the cheese has a unique portfolio of flavours, peaty, smoky with a hint of iodine. I like to think that these come from the draff, but whatever their origin Isle of Mull Cheddar makes a fine match with the Tobermory single malt.

# Keen's Cheddar

## Made by the Keen family in Somerset

 UNPASTEURISED COW'S MILK, ANIMAL RENNET

Keen's has a creamier texture than many Cheddars, and this higher moisture encourages more vigorous activity on the part of the starter bacteria, still working away in the cheeses as they mature. This higher level of bacterial activity results in the wilder flavours that a Keen's can show compared to its more sedate cousins in the Cheddar family. Acidity is more intense, more mouth-tingling, and there can be something spicy in a Keen's, a little hot, like mustard, with an intriguingly sulphuric tang.

As well as the imposing twenty-four-kilo cheeses – the common size of a traditional Cheddar, the Keen family make a twelve-kilo version. These shallower wheels, with their lower surface-to-mass ratio, have more of the flavour that comes from their cloth coats and the mould growing on top of those, the dank and earthy note that so reminds me of one of my favourite pastimes, wandering round a nice old country church. Taken together, these wilder and more forward flavours make eating Keen's a more intense experience. If the Cheddars of Britain and Ireland were an orchestra, then these big bold Keen's would be the brass section.

# Killeen

## Made by Marion Roeleveld in County Galway

PASTEURISED GOAT'S MILK, ANIMAL RENNET

Eminently multicultural, Killeen is made in Ireland by a Dutch woman from the milk of Swiss goats, a breed called Saarinen who, given their geographical origin, don't like too much sun. They fit right in in Ireland. Marion's partner Haske doesn't have a family background in agriculture but his relationship with goats goes way back. At the age of four, he asked his parents for a goat to which his father replied, 'You can have one when you can milk it.' So Haske went off to a local farm and started to learn and by five he had his first goat and at the age of fifteen he had built up a herd.

Killeen's size and hard texture – rare for a goat's cheese – allow it to be aged until its flavours become fantastically complex. I notice aromas of grass and butter, opening into earthiness, Marmite and an intimate goatiness, with a long finish of salty caramel. Great cheesemakers rely on their instincts and feelings as much as on instrument readings. If you ask Marion how she knows that the cheese is good, she says, 'When I taste it, and it is good, it makes me smile.'

# Kirkham's Lancashire

## Made by Graham Kirkham and his team in Lancashire

 UNPASTEURISED COW'S MILK, ANIMAL RENNET

Graham Kirkham left a career as a racing car mechanic to rejoin the family cheese business and learn his trade from his mother Ruth. Older Lancashire fans still call their classic cheese 'Mrs Kirkham's'. Made with raw milk from the family herd, cloth-bound and rubbed in butter, this mild yet complex cheese has sweet, buttery and pastry notes, gentle acidity, and an open fluffy texture that Graham describes as 'butter crumble'.

The Kirkham's texture is the result of a very specific and incredibly painstaking way of breaking up the curd with one's fingertips, and the complexity from a traditional way of making Lancashire in which curd produced over three days is blended before being put in the moulds – a method that will never be amenable to an economy of scale, but does produce excellent cheese.

The pastry flavour, savoury note and the acidic edge make Kirkham's a fine partner for sweet baked goods, a fact that Lancastrians acknowledge in the old saying 'An apple pie without cheese is like a kiss without a squeeze.'

# Kit Calvert Wensleydale

## Made at Hawes Creamery in Yorkshire

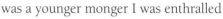 PASTEURISED COW'S MILK, ANIMAL RENNET

There are a lot of things that I love about this cheese, and one of them is its mildness and simplicity. When I was a younger monger I was enthralled by the big guns of the cheese world, the imposing farmhouse Cheddars and opulent Stiltons whose in-your-face flavours promised an intense experience. As I matured, I discovered the rarefied pleasures of more delicate cheeses, their reticent characters requiring a more mindful attitude to tasting. Wensleydale is an example of this lesson. If you are used to brash supermarket Cheddars you might discount it,  but you would be wrong. The clean milky flavour is lifted by a gentle acidity, and within it is an intriguing fresh green note like dill or cucumber.

This version of Wensleydale has some traditional aspects: the animal rennet confers creaminess and minimises bitterness, and the cheeses are formed into cylinders and bound in cloth. It is named for a local hero who ought to be celebrated more widely, a Dalesman who, with his rugged, ruthless determination, saved Wensleydale from the Depression, the Milk Marketing Board and, during the Second World War, the Ministry of Food. His name, may it live forever, was Kit Calvert.

# Lincolnshire Poacher

## Made by Simon and Tim Jones in Lincolnshire

UNPASTEURISED COW'S MILK, ANIMAL RENNET

Pineapple may not be a flavour you associate with a cheese, unless you grew up in the 1970s and remember the cheese hedgehog. However, it is a note often present in the Jones brothers' Lincolnshire Poacher, whose flavours and texture are as intriguing as its history, an instance of the cross-cultural fertilisation and innovation that characterised the Cheese Renaissance.

Poacher has the heft and the savoury notes of a Cheddar, and the dense texture and sweetness of a Swiss mountain cheese like Gruyère. The latter can be ascribed to the fact that Simon and Tim were originally taught cheesemaking by a much-loved figure of the Renaissance, the late Dougal Campbell, who learned his craft in the summer chalets high in the Swiss Alps. The sweetness is partly the result of a higher temperature make than would be traditional for a Cheddar. The cheeses are also dressed in a kind of waxy coating called plasticote instead of the traditional cloth, and this allows them to be matured for up to twice as long as a traditional Cheddar. As for the pineapple, even Poacher's makers aren't certain where that comes from, or how to replicate it consistently, a mystery that is a big part of the magic of cheese for me.

# Little Hereford

## Made by Karen and Mark Hindle in Herefordshire

🐄 UNPASTEURISED COW'S MILK, ANIMAL RENNET

Little Hereford was the first cheese Karen and Mark Kindle made when they started out in the 1990s, and is based on a recipe developed in 1918 by the Chief Dairying Instructress of the County of Hereford, Ellen Yeld. Ellen, despite her grandiose title, rode around the county on her bicycle helping local farmers to make cheese from their surplus milk, one assumes to this recipe, which fittingly for cheese made near the border with Wales is a sort of cross between Cheddar and Caerphilly. Ellen wrote a pamphlet on cheesemaking called *Practical Cheese-making for Smallholders, Farmers and Others*, and in 1917 was awarded an MBE for her services to cheesemaking during the austere days of the First World War, and quite right too. Little Hereford is named for the village where, in 1879, Ellen was born.

The Kindles' tribute cheese has an endearingly knobbly rind and the paste is a warm Cheddary yellow with an aroma of fresh straw. The texture is moist and flaky with an upfront acidity that mellows as the flavours develop. Next comes a clean savoury note that fills out into caramelised onion and melted cheese then, as if to clean the palate, the acidity returns, leaving a long pleasant sting in the mouth.

# Loch Arthur

## Made by Barry Graham and his team in Dumfries & Galloway

UNPASTEURISED COW'S MILK, VEGETARIAN RENNET

Loch Arthur is quite soft for a Cheddar, or Cheddar type, to use its maker's terminology. As an apprenticer monger I was taught to grade Cheddar by squeezing it between my fingertips, and back then I wanted to see them whiten under the pressure before I would bestow that noble name upon the cheese. My opinions have softened with age, and I am prepared to let more giving cheeses into the pantheon. Crucially, though, I want only a trace of moisture to remain on my fingertips, and this Loch Arthur does perfectly. The flavour is herbal and delicate with a light acidity that just tingles on the tip of my tongue. As the flavour develops, I find the acidity increases to a more spicy level, which is exciting.

In 1985, when Barry Graham decided to start making cheese, traditional farmhouse cheesemaking had died out in Scotland and he had to look up retired farmers to ask them about their cheesemaking. Barry was in at the beginning of the Cheese Renaissance, and was one of the founder members of the Specialist Cheesemakers Association, which for the last thirty years has championed the cause of British cheese.

# Lord of the Hundreds

## Made by the Delves family in Sussex

 UNPASTEURISED SHEEP'S MILK, VEGETARIAN RENNET

This cheese, based on a young or *semi-stagionato* Pecorino style, has a gentle honey aroma and a hint of old church from the white mould dusting its rind. The texture is open and crumbly yet retains a moist creaminess from the rich sheep's milk. Honey persists in the flavour along with grassiness, a note of toasted caramelised hazelnuts and a hint of lanolin.

Lord of the Hundreds, while not a traditional farmhouse cheese, has a noble pedigree which speaks both of centuries of cheesemaking history and the modern Cheese Renaissance. Sheep's milk was for centuries the dominant form of cheese in Britain, most of it made in indus-trial quantities in the medieval monasteries from the milk of their huge flocks. When the monasteries disappeared in the sixteenth century, so too did most sheep's milk cheese. The recipe for Lord of the Hundreds was originally developed by renaissance *affineur* and cheesemaker, the late James Aldridge, who with characteristic generosity gave the recipe to the Dyball family, who began making cheese in 2002. Maintaining James's legacy of gener-osity, as well as his cheese, in 2020 the Dyballs handed over the recipe to Joe Delves, who comes from a family of Sussex dairy farmers.

# Martell's Double Gloucester

## Made by Charles Martell in Gloucestershire

✿ UNPASTEURISED COW'S MILK, ANIMAL RENNET

Martell's Double Gloucester is a mighty cheese, with a velvety grey mould rind, a deep sunset orange coloured paste and an aroma of caramel and a hint of cow. The flavour is brothy, like a well-reduced beef stock, with a fruity note, and the fudgey mouth-coating texture is cut through with firm acidity. Taken together, the effect is of a rich gamey meat braised in a reduced citrus sauce, a sort of cheese version of duck *à l'orange*.

The difference between Double and Single Gloucester is contentious, and Charles Martell is happy to set the record straight. To make Single, he says, the cream was skimmed from the evening milk, then mixed with the morning milk and made to a fast low-acid recipe, resulting in softer, shorter-keeping cheese. The Double, made to a higher acid recipe, was harder, drier and could mature for longer into a more robustly flavoured cheese. This texture meant it could stand the trip by cart to London – where the cheese could command a higher price – and on ships as far away as the West Indies and America. Eighteenth- and nineteenth-century cheese factors (traders), robust fellows all, would jump up and down on the cheeses to test their fitness for the voyage.

# Mayfield

## Made by Arthur Alsop in Sussex

PASTEURISED COW'S MILK, VEGETARIAN RENNET

The gentle buttery aroma is deceptive – there's a lot going on in a Mayfield. It is coated in wax like a Gouda but, as its creator declares, it is essentially a cross between a Comté and Emmental. Indeed, it has some of the sweet nutty character you'd expect from Alpine cheese, along with hints of its British *terroir* and a singular texture. Flavours open with sweet cream and burnt sugar – so far so alpine – but as the springy Emmental-like texture breaks down into a mouth-coating cream I get beery maltiness, restrained hops – more British than West Coast – caramelised onion and, to top it off, a beefy savoury flavour more like Cheddar.

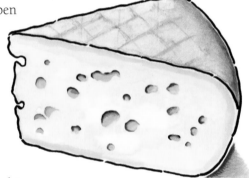

Even with such a broad range of flavours, Mayfield's overall character is still approachably mild and sweet. I once asked the head cheesemaker if he relied on instruments or instinct, to which he replied, 'Well, I knew the thermometer was bust one day when I put my hand in the vat and just knew that wasn't the right temperature.' Which answers that question. From the quality and complexity of his cheese, I'd say his instincts are good.

# Montgomery's Cheddar

## Made by Jamie Montgomery and Steve Bridges in Somerset

UNPASTEURISED COW'S MILK, ANIMAL RENNET

'Beefy' is a word often used to describe the umami flavour in a Monty's – as this cheese is affectionately known to its friends. 'Brothy' also comes to mind, both satisfying and comforting flavours, befitting a style of cheese so close to the British cheese fancier's heart. For all that beefiness, though, Monty's is not bold and brash, but shows a modest yet commanding restraint – it is the woodwind in the orchestra of British Cheddars – along with a profound complexity of flavour.

Like other proper farmhouse Cheddars, Monty's can show notes of hay and an earthy cellariness picked up during its long sojourn in the barn, where the cheeses – traditionally bound in cloth – develop an extra overcoat of grey mould. Their serried ranks stretching back into the dim recesses of the barn, these cheeses have the air of ancient stone artefacts, which seems right in the West Country, a region rich in reminders of our prehistoric past, including of course the most iconic monument in Britain, Stonehenge.

# Mossfield

## Made by Ralph Haslam in County Offaly

 PASTEURISED COW'S MILK, VEGETARIAN RENNET

Mossfield has that rich deep orange yellow you often see in a Gouda style, though that richness is as much to do with the quality of the pasture on Ralph's farm, which is on limestone, its diversity increased by his commitment to organic farming methods. The rind has a warm animal aroma as of a cow barn on a summer's day with a cabbagey hint, and the sweet caramel-flavoured paste shot through with a tingling acidity breaks down in the mouth into a luscious palate-coating texture. There is a surprise in store, however, since at twelve months, Mossfield has a scattering of amino acid crystals like umami-flavoured pop rocks hidden throughout the paste, whose crunch provides a delightful contrast to the creamy texture. At that age there is a definite bite to the flavour, which really brings out the sweetness in contrast.

Ralph also sells cheese at nine, or as young as six, months, where sweetness and a smooth buttery texture will be more to the fore.

# Norfolk Dapple

## Made by Ellie Betts and her team in Norfolk

UNPASTEURISED COW'S MILK, ANIMAL RENNET

'Glory be to God for dappled things,' says Gerard Manley Hopkins in his poem 'Pied Beauty', and with its sunset orange and russet flecked rind, he might have been talking about this cheese. It's cloth-bound, but I notice its makers don't call it a Cheddar, 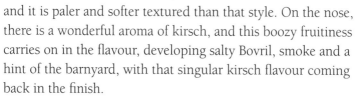 and it is paler and softer textured than that style. On the nose, there is a wonderful aroma of kirsch, and this boozy fruitiness carries on in the flavour, developing salty Bovril, smoke and a hint of the barnyard, with that singular kirsch flavour coming back in the finish.

The milk for Norfolk Dapple comes from a single farm nearby, called Abbey Farm, and the cows graze by the glorious ruins of Binham Priory, founded in the eleventh century by a nephew of William the Conqueror. Medieval East Anglia was famed for its cheesemaking and the farm's name suggests that it was a possession of the Priory. It's not too much of a stretch to think that cheese was made here for the monks' refectory, and if their old bones nourish the land that produces this lovely cheese I'm sure they'd be pleased at the thought.

# Old Winchester

## Made by Mike and Judy Smales and their team in Wiltshire

🐄 PASTEURISED COW'S MILK, VEGETARIAN RENNET

The Smales, who have been farming their land for fifty years, decided twenty years ago to 'dip their toe' in cheesemaking. They did a brief Cheddar-making course with venerated cheesemaker Val Bines but wisely chose not to go up against that established cheese and began instead with a Gouda recipe. Wanting to 'give their cheese an English accent', they made some changes, including washing the curd less to increase acidity and using different starters instead of traditional Gouda ones.

At the outset, the Smales had 'no great vision for where we were going', an exploratory attitude common to many great cheesemakers that can – as here – produce impressive results. Old Winchester gives off an enticing aroma of sweet buttered popcorn. The paste is a sunny yellow colour with a fissured texture and a scattering of small holes reminiscent of a Gouda. The texture is surprisingly moist, and in the mouth breaks down into a rich creaminess, born of a careful control of acidity during the make and equally careful and sensitive maturation. Caramelised sweetness is balanced by the acidic bite and beefy savouriness of Cheddar, with notes of warm moist hay and a pleasing astringent tingle in the long finish.

# Owd Ewe

## Made by Iona Hill in Yorkshire

UNPASTEURISED COW'S MILK, VEGETARIAN RENNET

The paste of Owd Ewe is straw yellow and has a light aroma of toasted corn. Its soft fudge texture melts in the mouth, releasing floral sweetness, a note of fresh hay and more of that toasted corn. The flavours are delicate and very clean, with just a savoury hint of sheepiness; the acidity is so gentle and well integrated that it is barely noticeable, serving to tie the flavours together and softening into a smooth creamy finish.

In her previous life, Iona Hill flew light aircraft into such noted tourist destinations as Balochistan and the Swat Valley in Northern Pakistan, before a chance encounter in South Africa with a mercenary officer who had a debt problem led her to a career in accounting. This background may not seem like an obvious lead into cheesemaking, except that I detect an adventurous attitude and a degree of grit, which are useful in such a demanding and uncertain business. Owd Ewe is descended from Iona's wax-covered Original Ewe. Wanting to make a natural rinded cheese that could be matured to develop more complex flavour, she tweaked the recipe such that the new cheese could 'thrive over time', which it certainly has.

# Pitchfork Cheddar

## Made by the Trethowan brothers in Somerset

🐄 UNPASTEURISED COW'S MILK, ANIMAL RENNET

Delicacy, restraint and balance are qualities that Pitchfork Cheddar, an accomplished and award winning cheese, quietly revels in, the result of a consistency of practice and attention to detail that would be pathological in anyone other than a cheesemaker. Another quality that the great cheesemaker requires is humility, one that Todd and Maugan Trethowan have in spades. Of their first ever batch of cheese, a traditional Caerphilly made on their family farm in West Wales, Todd said, 'I was just pleased it was even round'.

The flavour notes for this cheese are not what you would expect if you are used to 'mature' industrial Cheddar with its mouth-burning acidity and crunchy crystals but little in the way of complexity. The first note is sweetness. That swiftly fills out into a cooked milk caramel flavour, notes of lush grassy pasture; hay and earth follow, and a hint of butteriness. All of these, bound together with a backbone of restrained acidity, leave a pleasant tingle in the finish, persisting for a long while after the morsel is finished.

# Quicke's Cheddar

## Made by Mary Quicke and her team in Devon

PASTEURISED COW'S MILK, ANIMAL RENNET

Quicke's has an aroma of mossy woodland floor that, while in that spectrum of earth and cellar you expect to find in a cloth-bound Cheddar, is distinctive to this particular cheesemaker. Their mature cheese has sweet clean character, offering a lovely woody note, and the acidity is so gentle and well-intertwined with the flavours of the cheese as to be barely perceptible.

Mary Quicke makes older Cheddars, called extra-mature and vintage, which have a sharper acidity and are more forward, but with my penchant for balance and restraint the slightly younger mature is my favourite. The Quicke family are conscientious stewards of their woodlands, and rather pleasingly the boards the cheeses mature on are from trees which grew on the estate. This stewardship extends even to the quality and microfloral diversity of the soil. While this reflects Mary's responsibility as the fourteenth generation of her family to farm this land, it is also enlightened self-interest – the soil produces a rich and diverse crop that a happy and diverse herd of cows turn into excellent milk which Mary and her team, with a century of cheesemaking experience between them – turn into elegant and complex cheeses.

# St Andrews

## Made by Jane Stewart in Fife

🐄 UNPASTEURISED COW'S MILK, ANIMAL RENNET

Scottish Cheddars tend to be paler than their Welsh and English cousins. Short summers and a cooler wetter climate have their effect on the character of the grass, which in turn affects the colour, flavour and texture of the cheese. Excitingly, Scottish Cheddar *terroir* is even more fine grained than that, and the attentive cheese fancier can distinguish between east and west coast Cheddars. St Andrews, an east coast cheese, is paler than the sunset yellow of a Somerset Cheddar, but the

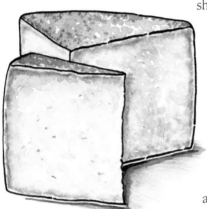

shade is a sort of biscuit or pale roux, rather than the blanched ivory of Isle of Mull, from the west coast, whose wetter climate and shorter grazing season makes for less rich pasture. St Andrews is a fairly high-moisture, soft-textured Cheddar, an environment in which ripening bacteria flourish and their vigorous activity produces a hefty aroma – winey with a pronounced note of the barnyard. The flavour opens with an upfront acidity which softens to a light tingling in the mouth, developing a fermented silage note, and finishing with toasted corn. Like its stablemate, Anster, this fascinating complex Cheddar reminds me of the eminently rustic French Cantal. It is a cheese of considerable authority.

# Saint Gall

## Made by Frank and Gudrun Shinnick in County Cork

UNPASTEURISED COW'S MILK, ANIMAL RENNET

Saint Gall signals its Alpinity with a supple paste scattered with holes, although the colour is quite rich for that style, reflecting the excellent pasture of County Cork. The aroma is sharp with notes of barnyard and hazelnuts, common to this style. Athough the flavour tends more towards the savoury than the sweet, I notice hot mustard, earth, barnyard and a meaty savoury note with some dark chocolate coming through later and an astringent tingle in the finish.

Gudrun Shinnick, originally from Germany, learned her cheesemaking there and in Switzerland, and Saint Gall has much in common with Appenzeller. At the same time, the Shinnicks cultivate their own starters from the milk from their farm, giving the cheese its own unique character. The name reflects this cross-cultural fermentation. Saint Gall was an Irish monk who lived as a hermit and preacher in what would become the Appenzell region of Switzerland. He went there as part of Saint Columbanus's mission to convert the pagans of the continent and – some Irish cheesemakers lay claim – to teach them how to make cheese. Saint Gall is also famous for persuading an angry bear to gather firewood and sit down companionably with him to share the warmth of the fire.

# Shropshire

## Made by Tom Humphris and Paul Bedford in Shropshire

🐄 PASTEURISED COW'S MILK, ANIMAL RENNET, KEFIR STARTER

This confidently named, cloth-bound cheese has a pale yellow colour and crumbly texture, suggesting the kind of fast, high acid make used for a Cheshire. The aroma is sweet with a slight hint of cow and the flavours are also reminiscent of Cheshire – minerality and a juicy acidity rounded out with a creamier buttery note. Fast developing acidity in the make can lead to a rather dry texture, and it's a mark of the cheesemakers' skill that they have kept that process in check such that the cheese has a lovely moist crumble texture.

More important, Shropshire has a character all of its own, a fermented tang like cider vinegar and a gently tingling astringency in the finish. This is due to the unique kefir starter, which (unlike a conventional culture) contains yeasts and acetic acid bacteria – which account for that cider vinegar flavour – as well as lactophilic cultures. It's easy to see why most cheesemakers don't use kefir in cheesemaking; it can produce 'wildly inconsistent results', according to Tom. But it also 'creates all the complexity', as well as the salty-sweet buttery flavour. The kefir is continuously cultured from the milk of their own herd, and expresses the unique character of the farm and its *terroir*.

# Sparkenhoe Red Leicester

## Made by David and Jo Clarke in Warwickshire

 UNPASTEURISED COW'S MILK, ANIMAL RENNET

Sparkenhoe is a truly traditional Red Leicester, cloth-bound and hand-made on the Clarkes' family farm with raw milk from their own herd.

When David and Jo Clarke started making this cheese in 2005 it was the first raw milk farmhouse Red Leicester to be made in Britain since the 1950s, and industrial versions had done so much damage to this cheese's reputation that it was even hard to get customers to try it. Thankfully this smashing cheese seems to have undone that damage single-handedly and is rightfully popular. The red colour, which comes from the traditional annatto dye, announces in advance to the happy cheese fancier what a comforting cheese this is, with its heart-warming mix of sweet and savoury flavours and rich chewy texture.

Like all the territorials, a family unique to British cheese-making and including such old favourites as Cheshire and Lancashire, Sparkenhoe is fairly mild and rewards mindful tasting to fully appreciate its depth and complexity. For a more intense experience you could try Sparkenhoe Vintage, which, at three times the age, is an understandably more forward cheese.

# Spenwood

## Made by Anne and Andy Wigmore in Berkshire

UNPASTEURISED SHEEP'S MILK, VEGETARIAN RENNET

Spenwood's pale colour, the shade of ivory, tells you that this is a sheep's or goat's' milk cheese – cow's milk gives a deeper yellow. The aroma is floral, with a hint of old stone, and the flavour has a forward acidity, balanced by a milky sweetness with just the right amount of salt coming through in the finish.

Like many British and Irish cheeses of the 1970s and 1980s, Spenwood was inspired by a continental cheese, in this case a chance encounter with some Sardinian Pecorino while Anne and Andy were on their way to Australia in a yacht.

Coincidentally, or not, Spenwood looks a lot to me like the kind of cheese that the Roman army was feeding its legionaries when they were quartered out here, and I believe that indigenous cheesemakers took note and gave the recipe a try.

You could do the same sort of thing with Spenwood as you would with Pecorino – make pesto out of it or grate it on pasta. Or just enjoy a piece with a glass of wine. An off-dry oxidised Malvasia from Sardinia would be delicious, and geographically appropriate.

# Summerfield

## Made by Alastair Pearson and his team in North Yorkshire

UNPASTEURISED COW'S MILK, VEGETARIAN RENNET

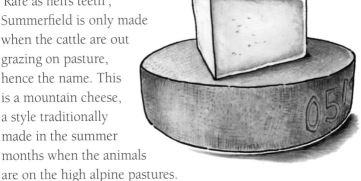

'Rare as hen's teeth', Summerfield is only made when the cattle are out grazing on pasture, hence the name. This is a mountain cheese, a style traditionally made in the summer months when the animals are on the high alpine pastures. Typical examples include Swiss Gruyère or French Comtè, but Alastair Pearson learned his craft in Germany where they make a family of cheeses called Bergkäse ('mountain cheese').

Alastair's cattle are Dairy Shorthorn, a traditional British breed that give excellent milk, high in butterfat, much like the milk from the Swiss Browns and Montbeliardes that goes into making alpine cheese. With their concave sides and horizontal cracks their cheeses look like their continental cousins and the flavour, all nuts and caramels with a little hay and just a hint of the barnyard, is eminently mountainous.

Botton Village, where Summerfield is made, is a community for adults with learning difficulties, part of the Camphill Movement which was started in 1939 by Austrian refugees from Nazism. The community farms bio-dynamically, a holistic system that emphasises animal and soil health, and biodiversity. You can't make great cheese unless you're a decent human being. This is an outstanding cheese.

# Teifi

## Made by John Savage-Onstwedder and team in Ceredigion

⚜ UNPASTEURISED COW'S MILK, ANIMAL RENNET

John Savage-Onstwedder and his partner Paula came to Wales from the Netherlands in 1982. It's no accident that they chose Ceredigion to settle in, for the county's rich pastures are ideal for dairy farming. Teifi, named for the river that borders part of the county, is based on a Gouda recipe, but has its own unique character.

The aroma of a younger Teifi is buttery, with a cheesy edge, and is more savoury than Gouda, with a bright acidity and just a hint of caramel in the finish. Mature Teifis are sweeter, and with an unexpectedly creamy texture – I would expect aged Gouda styles to be much harder. The older cheese has more acidic bite, a heady sweetness and a hint of caramelised onion in the finish. The vat is a Dutch one made of teak rather than copper or steel, and this reflects a traditional method of heating the curd. Instead of direct heat from a fire or a steam jacket, some of the whey is run off and hot water added to the curd. This produces a dense pliable texture and a sweeter flavour.

The family also make a single malt called Dà Mhìle, which is aged in whisky casks and has a smooth sweet flavour that makes it an excellent partner for this fine cheese.

# Templegall

## Made by Dan Hegarty and Jean-Baptiste Enjelvin in Co. Cork

 UNPASTEURISED COW'S MILK, ANIMAL RENNET

There is a lot going on with this imposing Gruyère-style cheese. Its name is an anglicised version of *An Teampall Geal*, the Irish name of the nearby village of Whitechurch. In its English form this name hints fortuitously at the possible monastic origin of Alpine cheese and the Irish Saint Gall in whose name a famous monastery was established in Switzerland. The cheese is made in a sixty-year-old copper vat, but unlike its continental relatives, which are made from the creamy milk of Montbéliarde cattle, Templegall is made from the milk of the Hegartys' Friesian cows, at no loss to its dense rich texture.

As with Alpine cheeses, Jean-Baptiste only makes cheese when the cows are on pasture – silage fed milk is not used for Alpine cheese. And, to unleash a further bit of Alpine cheese geekery on you, 'Gruyère' can refer to a single Swiss AOP cheese, or to a family that includes Comté and 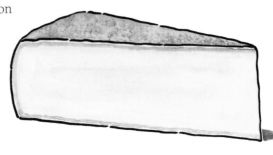 Beaufort, widely acknowledged as two of the greatest cheeses in the world. Templegall, which reminds me most of Beaufort, has an aroma of malted milk with an animal edge: the dense texture breaks down and fills the mouth, giving sweet, nutty grassy flavours like a late summer hayfield.

# Tinto

## Made by Angela Cairns and the Erringtons in Lanarkshire

⚜ UNPASTEURISED GOAT'S MILK, VEGETARIAN RENNET

Hard goat's cheeses are difficult to make well – they tend towards bitterness and dryness – and are thus quite rare. Mary Holbrook, the godmother of British goat's cheese, used to make one called Old Ford, and when we lost Mary, who died in 2019, we also lost her cheese. Tinto, while described by the Erringtons as a semi-hard style, hardens and intensifies with age, which is why I've included it in this section. An aged Tinto is a worthy successor to Old Ford, and happily swells the ranks of hard goat's cheeses. It's a fascinating cheese. I get an aroma of candlenuts – fatty, macadamia-like nuts with a hint of almond. The salting is up-front – another reminder of Mary, who loved salt – but takes a back seat as the other flavours develop: more of that nuttiness, a just detectable sweetness.

Despite what I've said about older goat's cheeses developing more goatiness, I can't really detect that controversial flavour. Perhaps it is there, but subsumed in the mix of this accomplished and delicious cheese.

# Wells Alpine

## Made by Catherine Temple in Norfolk

🐄 PASTEURISED COW'S MILK, VEGETARIAN RENNET

You don't get many mountains in Norfolk, but what you do get is a herd of Swiss Brown cows, a very talented cheesemaker and a cheese that, while not as supple sweet or nutty as a Gruyère or a Comté, does have a fascinating mix of Alpine and British qualities. Wells Alpine, named for the nearby town of Wells-next-the-Sea, is the same shape as an Alpine cheese, although the paste is a richer yellow and has a more Cheddar-like openness to it than the smooth texture of a Gruyère. I get a savoury aroma of Dijon mustard and grass, and the flavour is buttery and sweet with a crystalline crunch that signifies the presence of crystallised aminoacid and adds a tasty umami flavour. The cheese has a very clean flavour and, while it starts out buttery and gentle, there is a long slow buildup of acidity which reaches an intense tingling finale at the finish.

Catherine Temple was already making a range of cheeses from their herd of Friesian-Holsteins when a chance encounter with some local cheese on an Alpine cycling holiday gave her the idea to try making this style, and so she and her husband bought the Swiss Browns, showing the kind of commitment you need to make really great cheese.

# Westcombe Cheddar

## Made by Tom Calver and his team in Somerset

UNPASTEURISED COW'S MILK, ANIMAL RENNET

Westcombe has all the depth and complexity you would expect from a cloth-bound raw milk Cheddar, with notes of grass, fresh hay, beefy umami and cellary earthiness, brightened with a delicate acidity. The cheese is relatively mild, which can be a bit of a surprise to a palate used to commercially produced Cheddars, where intensity tends to compensate for a lack of complexity, requiring a bit of a reset as to what Cheddar actually is.

The Calver family have actually performed this reset in that they returned to traditional cloth-bound cheesemaking in the early 1990s after a period of making pasteurised block on the farm. In the last few years Tom has changed his recipe again, to one the seminal nineteenth-century Cheddar maker Edith J. Cannon would recognise, producing a softer-textured cheese whose gentleness allows the complex flavours to shine. This move is not just a nod to cheesemaking history but acknowledges an impressive pedigree, for Edith used to make cheese on Tom's farm. Tom is not a slave to tradition, however. The cheeses in his cavernous store are looked after by a cheese-turning robot called, affectionately, Tina-the-Turner.

# Cheese Board

# Cheese Board

Choosing cheese . . . . . . . . . 217
Tasting cheese . . . . . . . . . . . 218
How much to buy . . . . . . . . 220
How long to keep cheese. . . 220
A great cheesseboard . . . . . . 221
Serving cheese . . . . . . . . . . . 221
What to drink with cheese . 224
A little Welsh rarebit . . . . . . 225
Index of cheesemakers . . . . 228
Index of cheeses . . . . . . . . . 231
Cheese gazetteer . . . . . . . . . 235

# Choosing cheese

The cheeses that most interest me are those that are made on a small scale, on a farm or in a dairy that uses locally bought milk and where the methods used are informed by tradition.

Your best bet for finding such cheeses is an actual cheese shop, a deli, or perhaps a dedicated cheese counter in a supermarket. Having found your promising shop, the next thing to ensure is that the cheeses on offer look happy and healthy. Beware of the following:

● **Heavily-cracked surfaces** hint that a cheese has dried out – a sign of age, overly dry conditions or inadequate wrapping.

● **Hard cheeses with patches of mould** on the cut surface might mean the shop is too damp or the cheeses have been under wraps for too long, or haven't had their exposed surfaces trimmed to keep them nice and fresh looking, a process mongers call 'facing.'

● **Brownish layers between rind and paste** tell you that the cheeses have gone too long without facing or simply denote a cheese that is a little past its best.

Clingfilm is a blessing and a curse. It is excellent at holding in moisture, and will prevent the surface of a cheese drying and cracking. At the same time, it holds in moisture, which can cause unwanted mould growth and pappy texture. The best way to avoid the latter is to use clingfilm sparingly, ideally just wrapping the cut face and leaving the rind open and free to breathe. This can be done so skilfully that the clingfilm layer is barely visible, which we mongers call glass wrapping. Smaller pieces are difficult to wrap like this and may need to be entirely covered. In this case, I like to see that the cheeses under their wrapping still look bright and fresh, free of unwanted mould or discolouration. This pleasing appearance will be because they have been regularly unwrapped, faced and wrapped again, a constant process in any good cheese shop or counter.

## TASTING CHEESE

Having looked and seen that it is good, you will now want to taste some cheese. Cheeses change from batch to batch as the weather changes and the seasons turn, and unless you are in a tearing hurry, and really trust your cheesemonger, you should always taste before you buy. There is a way to taste cheese mindfully, when buying it, and indeed when tasting your way through a cheeseboard. This is how.

First, observe your cheese – you can tell a lot from how a cheese looks. Much of this is about the type of cheese: a pink or orange rind indicates a washed-rind, goat's milk cheeses are white, cow's milk cheeses are sunny yellow, and so on. This sort of thing isn't all that informative, especially if there are labels, though being able to spot a goat's cheese on a cheeseboard might impress your friends. Over time, though, you will come to recognise visual clues to the sorts of flavours and textures you like. For example, a *narrow breakdown* on a Camembert style tells you that the cheese is young and fresh tasting, whereas a uniformly creamy paste signals the cheese is fully broken down and will be more intense. I like both, myself.

The next thing is to squeeze your cheese. Feel the level of moisture on rind and paste, and give it a gentle squeeze to test the texture. I look for a Goldilocks point of moisture – enough to leave a slight trace on my fingertips, yet not so much that my fingers feel greasy. The correct texture depends on the type of cheese. Cheddar ought to offer some resistance; fresh goat's cheeses ought not to be dry and hard. (Obviously you'd never do this, but please don't try and squeeze the cheeses on the counter; cheesemongers don't like it when you do that. But they will generally give you a sample to try.)

Now give the cheese a smell, just as if you are tasting wine. Since our tastebuds only register sweet, sour, salty, bitter and umami, all the really interesting stuff happens with aroma. Try to name the aromas, perhaps even out loud with your cheesemonger, as it will focus your attention and the act of labelling will over time improve your ability to separate out and identify different ones. Don't be afraid to say the first thing that comes to mind, however absurd it might sound: bubblegum, biscuit, leather, pencil shavings are all notes I have found in cheese, as you may have noticed in the book.

Now, finally, it is time to eat some cheese. A good cheese, just like a good wine, should have a progression of flavours that develop over time in the mouth, a beginning, a middle and a finish; a narrative structure of flavour, if you will. Pay attention to what's happening over time. What's the first flavour you notice? What does that develop into as the cheese warms in your mouth, and what is the finish?

There should be some *length*; that is to say, the final flavour should persist for a while after the cheese itself is gone. Length is for me one of the key indicators of quality in a cheese. Even a cheese with a very intense upfront flavour can fade to nothing all too swiftly.

I value complexity in a cheese, but there are many outstanding cheeses with a simple flavour, and balance is more important. For example, while I like a nice tingle of acidity in a Cheddar, I don't want that to overwhelm all the other flavours in its palette. Again, I would talk about what you're tasting as you taste it – having swallowed first, of course – and resist the urge to self-censor. Your subconscious is good at this.

# HOW MUCH TO BUY?

Obviously this depends on what you're doing with your cheese. For an after-dinner cheeseboard, I'd offer at least 30 grams of each cheese per person, and round up a bit in case of hungry guests. When I'm buying my weekly cheese I buy larger amounts, even though there are only two of us at home. I might get a whole Dorstone goat weighing in at around 180 grams, a 300-gram hunk of Cheddar and the same of Stilton. These would still be in good condition a week later, although in our house they'd be long gone, having appeared on cheeseboards, in sandwiches and salads, or just snacked on while I cook.

Christmas is, as we all know, all about the cheese, and I like to really let myself go. Last year I bought six kilos of cheese for the family cheeseboard – equal amounts of Stichelton, Pitchfork Cheddar and Kirkham's Lancashire – and that kept ten of us happy for more than a week.

Keep your cheese in the salad drawer of the fridge wrapped in the waxed paper they ought to have come in. Being more enclosed, the drawer protects your cheeses from the drying action of the fan, yet allows them to breathe more easily than they would in a closed Tupperware box. If there are vegetables in there, so much the better; they act as humidifiers. But don't leave a cut onion or anything else strong smelling in with your cheese, as the fat in the cheese will take up the flavour.

## HOW LONG TO KEEP CHEESE

'How long can I keep a cheese for?' must be one of the longest answer questions that mongers get asked. It's complicated. For cheese doesn't go off so much as change. The best-before date – if there is one – is more of a guideline, telling you when the cheesemaker or monger thinks the cheese to be still at its best.

*Older, lower-moisture cheeses* will change less, and larger pieces, with more mass-to-surface area, will also change more slowly. I have enjoyed *hard cheeses* like Cheddar or Red Leicester for weeks, although admittedly they began as pretty huge chunks.

At the other end of the spectrum, a *young fresh cheese* like Cote Hill White is best eaten in the few days after you bought it, which is fine because it's small. *Mould-ripened*, *Blue* and *Washed-rind* cheeses will ripen slowly, increasing in flavour and intensity.

If you see unfamiliar *moulds* growing on the surface of your cheese, just give it a scrape; what's underneath will taste fine.

I would really prefer it if you didn't freeze your cheese, as long as you keep it wrapped in the way I've described. I find that freezing any cheese changes the texture such that it is no longer welcome on my cheeseboard.

Of course, the quality of your cheese can go down as well as up, and your cheese can become tired and muted as it loses the fresh bloom of youth. It's really up to you to decide when your cheese has lost its zing or is getting a bit much. At this point the time has come to retire it from the cheeseboard and do something else with it (see 'A little Welsh rarebit', below). But don't just throw it away!

## A GREAT CHEESEBOARD

For a great cheeseboard, you want a range of textures and flavours, but just three well-chosen and decently sized cheeses will cover that. I prefer a few good-sized pieces, rather than a fancy array. I might start with a *mild soft cow's milk*, like Saint Jude, then a *hard sheep's cheese* with a bit more complexity like the Irish Cais Na Tire, and finish with something more characterful like the Erringtons' *goats cheese*, Lanark Blue. Notice that in this small but perfectly formed selection there is a variety of textures, flavours and animal sources. The above is also the order in which I would eat these cheeses, progressing from the milder to the more intense flavours, and that's a general principle for tasting cheese. If you started with the Lanark Blue, the Saint Jude might seem a bit muted by comparison.

With this limited selection I have chosen relatively mild cheeses, so that friends with more delicate palates don't miss out. For a larger cheeseboard I might include one or two *wilder cheeses*, like the Welsh Saval, with its barnyardy bouquet, or a sulphurously-ripe Tunworth. I'd also include some more *styles of cheese*, for example a proper cloth-bound Cheddar like Montgomery's or Quicke's, perhaps Baron Bigod (a *Brie-style* cheese from Norfolk) and a *soft goat's cheese* like the pyramidical Sinodun Hill. Even if someone found one or two cheeses a bit too intense, there would still be plenty of other cheeses for them to enjoy.

If your friends are cheese geeks, or simply enthusiastic gourmets, you could present a selection of cheeses of the *same* family. For example, you could serve a cheeseboard made up entirely of *blues*. I'd begin with the buttery Cashel, then go on to the more complex Beenleigh; I'd have Stilton, of course, and a rare blue goat's like Lanark, and might end on a strong finish with the eminently rustic Hebridean Blue. This selection still has all the variety of flavour, texture and animal of the three-cheese board.

Less challenging but equally fascinating would be a cheeseboard of *territorials* – a family of milder hard cow's cheeses unique to the British Isles. Start with a creamy herbaceous Wensleydale like Kit Calvert or the farmhouse-style Stonebeck, and then move to the moistly crumbly Appleby's Cheshire with its delicate mineral edge. Don't forget good farmhouse Red Leicester, nor Caerphilly, of course, or Lancashire, and Single Gloucester really ought to be more widely celebrated than it is. Maybe finish with a big beefy cloth-bound Cheddar, and then spend the rest of the night arguing with your friends about whether Cheddar really is a territorial.

On the vexed question of before or after pudding, I am with the French – you want to have your cheese before pudding when your appetite is still un-sated and your perceptions sharper. Cheese time is for mindful tasting and talking about the aromas and flavours, focusing your attention, and improving your ability to pick out and identify flavours. It is also fun.

## SERVING CHEESE

Cheese tasting works best at room temperature, so get your cheeses out of the fridge about an hour before you want to eat them. When you unwrap a cheese, you might see a film of moisture or a dulled sheen on the cut face. This will have a slightly tired flavour, so whenever I get cheese out of the fridge I give the face a light scrape with a sharp knife. A light dusting of mould on the surface is fine, too – just clear it away with a light scrape. (Dogs will appreciate these shavings).

Cutting cheese is a discipline in itself, but there is one principle that holds true for all shapes and sizes, which is that everyone should get an equitable distribution of rind and paste. Imagine a classic disc-shaped cheese like a Camembert. Each person should cut themselves a wedge-shaped pie slice going from the centre to the outside of the cheese. If your piece of cheese is already in a wedge and is broad enough, you can divided it into smaller pie slices, but for a narrow wedge that can get tricky. My solution is to lay the cheese on its flat side and cut pieces from what was the top until you get to the rind. Do not cut off the pointy end of a wedge, the nose. In northern England this heinous act is referred to as *snebbing*, and getting a reputation as a snebber will cut down on your dinner invites.

*Accompaniments* ought to be chosen as mindfully as your cheeses. Grapes are a common sight on a cheeseboard, but an acidic green grape with an acidic

Caerphilly is an awful lot of acid. I would match acidic cheeses with a sweeter fruit like a ripe fig, and luscious creamy cheeses with something tart. So those green grapes might go well with a *triple-crème* like Elmhirst. Cheeses high in salt and umami, the washed-rinds and blues, reward pairing with sweetness; so try a sticky red

onion marmalade with a fulsome washed-rind like Milleens.

*Biscuits* should be plain or at most mildly flavoured – oatcakes, Swedish-style rye crackers – and the faithful Carr's water biscuit are favourites of mine. *Sourdough* bread with its tartness and chewy crust is a friend to cheeses everywhere.

## WHAT TO DRINK WITH CHEESE

The pairing of booze with cheese is a big subject. First off, you don't need to match each cheese on your board with a different wine. It is possible to pick just one that will go with most of the cheeses you're serving. Now this may come as a surprise, but *red wine* is not the ideal partner for every type of cheese in the world. The tannins in red can react with the fat to give an odd texture and, particularly for mould-rinds, a bitter flavour. Heftier reds can also overwhelm all but the most robust of cheeses. If I really wanted a red with my cheese, I would choose a gentle wine with low or softer tannin –

a Beaujolais or a younger Pinot Noir perhaps. But it's much easier to find a *white wine* that will match a range of cheeses, and my pick for an all-purpose cheese wine is one with some weight, balanced acidity, and a little sweetness, like a late-bottled Riesling or a Pinot Gris.

Even with a single wine and a selection of cheese, it's interesting and fun to think about which pairings work best, and which don't. And, of course, if your bank balance and your constitution are up for it, you could pick several different wines to go with your cheese. With both those ideas in mind, here are my fundamental principles for matching wine, or other booze, with cheese.

The first requirement for a pairing is that both cheese and drink are of similar intensity. The way to check this is to taste both at once, and then wait for a while. If neither one drowns out the other, they are well matched. After that, there are three ways to think about how a pairing might work. The first is by contrast, where the difference between the flavours makes one or both stand out more clearly. Try pairing the citrusy goat's cheese Dorstone with a Beaujolais – the acidity of the cheese makes the jammy fruit flavours in the wine pop. Flavours can also be complimentary, such that they work together. For example, the floral element of an Argentine Torrontés can intertwine rather beautifully with the hay note in a Westcombe Cheddar.

Finally, think about mouthfeel – how the textures of cheese and drink interact. This can lead to some exciting pairings. One of my favourite combinations is a sparkling wine with a soft cheese like the Camembert-style Tunworth, which in the mouth combine in a tingling mousse.

Don't get stuck on wine, either. Beer and cheese pairings are a whole world to explore. *Porter and Stilton* is one of my favourite matches of all time; West Country *cider and Cheddar* grow together and go together; and *whisky and cheese* matching can lead you into some memorable evenings.

## A LITTLE WELSH RAREBIT

The idea that a fine cheese is too good for cooking isn't one I subscribe to. I use the best olive oil I can afford, the freshest spices and the happiest meat I can find. So why wouldn't I do that with my cheese? I usually have two or three cheeses as store cupboard staples, as the basis of a quick meal. A heroic piece of Cheddar, or another long-keeping hard cow's cheese is a necessity, and simply in a sourdough sandwich with some farmhouse butter, vine tomatoes and a sprinkling of Maldon salt makes a meal fit for a king, or queen. Elizabeth I certainly thought so, saying, 'A meal of bread, cheese and beer constitutes the perfect food,' which is less famous than some of her other quotes, but no less inspiring. Parmesan for grating over pasta, adding to a soufflé, or as a simple but showy starter with slices of pear and a glass of Prosecco, is also a must. Since we are in British mode, you could substitute Parmesan in any of these roles with a hard sheep like Berkswell from Warwickshire or the Scottish Corra Linn.

*Fresh cheeses* make a great and longer-keeping alternative to crème fraîche, so I often have some of that in the fridge. Perroche – a fresh goat's cheese – and smoked salmon pasta feels hugely indulgent and is easy and quick to make. You could also drop some Perroche into your borscht in place of Russian smetana.

Cupboard staples aside, some truly wonderful meals have cheese as the centrepiece. *Fondue* needs no explanation, and one could use a mix of cheeses from the British Isles, like Lincolnshire Poacher, the Irish Templegall and the funky Ogleshield, in place of Alpine cheese. Ogleshield is a *raclette* style, so make *raclette* with it, which is cheese melted over boiled new potatoes and served with crunchy gherkins. Or try *tartiflette* – potatoes, bacon bits, cream, butter *and* cheese baked in the oven. But go for a run first.

For all that I have made a fuss about top-quality ingredients, cooking is a great way to use up cheese that has gone a bit far. For an elderly goat's cheese, once soft and fresh and now hard and intense, try shaving some into a green salad or just onto some toasted sourdough with a drop of olive oil. *Cheese on toast* must be the most obvious form of cheese cookery, and it's fun to grate a mix of hard cheeses for this rather than just using one type. *Welsh rarebit* is the posh form, in which you make a sauce with roux, grated cheese and beer. Traditional recipes call for ale and Cheddar, but I am just as happy with a mongrel mix of cheese and whatever ends of old booze are lying around.

*Béchamel sauce* made with various grated ends of hard cheese is delicious and in our house many cauliflower cheeses, fish pies and potato bakes have been enlivened in this way.

For *end-stage cheese*, and this may only be for cheese geeks and other crazy people, there is *fromage fort* – 'strong cheese'. This is a product only the French could have come up with. Take all the cheese you wish to retire, trim off and discard the gnarliest-looking parts (dried or ammoniated rinds or weird brown bits), chop the remainder into small pieces and blend them with some white wine, a little garlic and pepper, and a very small pinch of cayenne pepper. I use a blender to get a smooth paste, but you could do this by hand for a more rustic texture. The result is a cheese spread of considerable authority. Traditionally, French *fromagers* (cheesemongers) would keep this unrefrigerated in an earthenware pot, removing the lid and stirring from time to time to perfume their shop, but this would create a very strong cheese indeed, so you might be better off keeping it in the fridge. Spread *fromage fort* on bread, or even add a little to a cheese sauce when you are cooking. The French take it in the morning, displaying impressive fortitude, but even they moisten their mouths with a little black coffee first so that the cheese does not burn their mouth.

# Index of Cheesemakers

Adams Family
(Carmarthenshire). . . . 39, 153
Alsop, Arthur (Sussex) . . 48, 196
Appleby Family, and Garry Gray
(Shropshire) . . . . . . . . . . . 166
Bell Family
(Yorkshire). . . . . 24, 76, 78, 91
Betts, Ellie (Norfolk) . . . . . . 199
Biggane, Tom and Lena
(Co. Cork) . . . . . . . . . . . . 171
Blunt, Kevin and Alison
(Sussex) . . . . . . . . . . . . 44, 45
Bradley, Elizabeth
(Co. Carlow). . . . . . . . . . . 133
Bridges, Steve (Somerset) . . 197
Brooke's Dairy
(Monmouthshire) . . . . . . . . 34
Burgess, Tom (Co. Carlow) . 172
Burt, Claire (Cheshire) . . . . . . 79
Butlers Farmhouse Cheese
(Lancashire) . . . . . . . . . . . . 92
Cahalan, Barry and Lorraine
(Co. Tipperary). . . . . . . . . 169
Cairns, Angela, and the
Erringtons (Lanarkshire) . . 87
Calver, Tom (Somerset) 138, 214
Cheyney, Julie (Suffolk) 51, 122
Clarke, David and Jo
(Warwickshire) . . . . . . . . . 207

Clarke, Will (Warwickshire) . . 95
Clough, Gillian (Yorkshire). . . 46
Cooney, Paddy and Kay
(Co. Tipperary). . . . . . . . . 177
Craske Family (Gwent). . . . . . 22
Crickmore, Jonny (Norfolk) .. 35
Cropp, Silke and Tom
(Co. Cavan) . . . . .38, 40, 179
Crump, Jonathan
(Gloucestershire) . . . 136, 175
Cryer, Ceri (Wiltshire) . . . . . 155
Davenport Family
(Lincolnshire) . . . . 20, 82, 113
Davies Family (Dorset) . . . . . . 85
Delves Family (Sussex). . . . . 194
Dorward, Ann
(Ayrshire) . . . . . . . 19, 33, 180
Errington Family (Lanarkshire)
. . . . . . . . . . . 43, 87, 174, 212
Evans, Linda
(Pembrokeshire) . . . . . . . 132
Fairbairn, Carolyn
(Cumbria). . . . . . . . . 164, 176
Ferguson, Giana (Co. Cork) ..111
Fergusson, Marcus
(Somerset) . . . . . . . . . . . . 121
Finlay, George and Hanna
(Co. Wicklow) . . . . . . . . . . 18

Finlay, Wilma and David, and Stephen Palmer (Dumfries and Galloway) . . . . . . . . . 146

Finnegan, Michael (Co. Louth)77

Flanagan, Michael (Co. Mayo) 148

Fletcher Family(Warwickshire) . 167

Gill, Jeffa (Co. Cork). . . 108, 139

Gott, Martin (Cumbria) 123, 135

Graham, Barry (Dumfries & Galloway) . . . . . . . . . . . . 193

Grimond, Rose (Oxfordshire) . . . . 36, 62, 112

Grubb Family (Co. Tipperary) . . . . . . . 80, 83

Harris, Ben, and Robin Congdon (Devon) . . . . . . . . . . . . . . 73

Haslam, Ralph (Co. Offaly). . 198

Hattan Andrew and Sally (Yorkshire) . . . . . . . . . . . 150

Hawes Creamery (Yorkshire)..190

Hedges, Stacey, and Charlotte Spruce (Hampshire) . . . 58, 61

Hegarty, Dan, and Jean-Baptiste Enjelvin (Co. Cork). . 185, 211

Hempenstall, John and Bernie (Co. Wicklow) . . . . . . . 59, 97

Hill, Iona (Yorkshire) . . 182, 201

Hindle, Karen and Mark (Herefordshire) . ..75, 143, 192

Holden Family (Ceredigion). 183

Holton, Dave (Kent) . . . . . . . 109

Humphris, Tom, and Paul Bedford (Shropshire). . 55, 89, 93, 206

Jenner, Lyn and Jenny (Sussex) 50

Jennings Family (Pembrokeshire) . . . . 107, 170

Jones, Menai (Anglesey) . . . . . 90

Jones, Simon and Tim (Lincolnshire) . . . . . . . . . . 191

Jowett, David (Gloucestershire) . 114

Keen Family (Somerset) . . . . 187

Kevan, Billy (Nottinghamshire) 81, 94

Kirkham, Graham (Lancashire) . . 189

Lochhead, Gavin and Jane (Dumfries and Galloway). . . 21

Lonergan, Eamonn (Co. Waterford) . . . . . . . 181

Longman, Roger (Somerset) . . . . 47, 56, 110, 120

Martell, Charles (Gloucestershire) 125, 142, 195

Maxwell, Maggie (Northumberland) 84, 105, 137, 178

Mead, Carine (Cornwall) . . . 134

Montgomery Jamie, and Tim Giffey (Somerset) . . . 118, 197

Morgan, Peter (Dorset) . . . . . 184

Mumford, Debbie (Devon) . . 42, 154

Ni Ghairbhith, Siobhán (Co. Clare) . . . . . . . . . 52, 53

Noblet, Clare and Tom (Cumbria). . . . . . . . . . . . 140

Olianas, Mario (Yorkshire) . . 88, 156

Oglethorpe, Bill (London) . .168

Padfield, Hugh (Somerset) . . 71, 116

Pearson, Alastair (Yorkshire) 144, 209

Pouget, Baron Roger (Oxfordshire) . . . . . . . 92, 119

Quicke, Mary (Devon) . . . . . 203

Reade Family (Argyll and Bute) . 86, 186

Ridley, Andy (Lancashire). . . 147

Reade Family
(Isle of Mull) . . . . . . . . 86, 186
Ridley, Andy (Lancashire) . . . 147
Rimes, Carrie (Gwynedd) . . . . 37
Roeleveld, Marion
(Co. Galway) . . . . . . . . . . 188
Rose, Sandy and Andy
(Berkshire) . . . . . . . . . . . . 70
Salisbury, Katharine and
Jason (Suffolk) . . . . . . . . . 152
Savage-Onstwedder, John
(Ceredigion) . . . . . . . 124, 210
Schneider, Joe
(Nottinghamshire) . . . . . . . 96
Seator, Anne (Orkney) . . . . . 149
Sedli, Julianna, and Karim Niazy
(Wiltshire) . . . . . . . . . . . . 106
Sheridans (Co. Waterford) . . 181
Shinnick, Frank and Gudrun
(Co. Cork) . . . . . . . . . . . . 205
Skailes, Robin, and Howard
Lucas (Nottinghamshire). . . 72

Smales, Mike and Judy
(Wiltshire) . . . . . . . . 151, 200
Spence Family (Yorkshire) . . 145
Steele, Quinlan (Co. Cork) . 117
Stewart, Jane (Fife) . . . . 165, 204
Temple, Catherine
(Norfolk) . . . . . . . . . . 74, 213
Thomson, Michael
(Co. Down) . . . . . . . . . . . . 98
Trethowan brothers
(Somerset) . . . . . . . . 141, 202
van den Dikkenberg, Geurt
(Co. Tipperary) . . . . . . 80, 83
Westhead, Charlie
(Herefordshire) . . . . 23, 41, 49
Wigmore, Anne and Andy
(Berkshire) . . . . . 60, 115, 208
Willems, Dickie (Co. Cork) . 173
Wilson, Jason and Nina
(Orkney). . . . . . . . . . . . . . 126
Wright Family (Co. Armagh) . 57
Yarrow, Rachel, and Fraser
Norton (Oxfordshire) . . . . . 54

# Index of cheeses

## A

Admiral Collingwood
WASHED-RIND/COW ............ 105
Ailsa Craig MOULD-RIPENED/GOAT 33
Allerdale HARD/GOAT ............ 164
Angiddy MOULD-RIPENED/COW .... 34
Anster HARD/COW ................ 165
Appleby's Cheshire HARD/COW. 166

## B

Ballyhubbock Sheep's
Halloumi FRESH/SHEEP ......... 18
Barkham Blue BLUE/COW .......... 70
Baron Bigod MOULD-RIPENED/COW 35
Baronet WASHED-RIND/COW ..... 106
Bath Blue BLUE/COW .............. 71
Beauvale Blue BLUE/COW ......... 72
Beenleigh Blue BLUE/SHEEP ...... 73
Berkswell HARD/SHEEP .......... 167
Bermondsey Hard Pressed
HARD/COW .................... 168
Binham Blue BLUE/COW .......... 74
Bix MOULD-RIPENED/COW ......... 36
Blue Monk BLUE/COW ............. 75
Bluemin White BLUE/COW ........ 76
Boyne Valley Blue BLUE/GOAT .... 77
Brefu Bach
MOULD-RIPENED/SHEEP ........ 37
Buffalo Blue BLUE/BUFFALO ...... 78
Burt's Blue BLUE/COW ............ 79

## C

Caerfai Caerffili
SEMI-SOFT/COW ................ 132
Cais Na Tire HARD/SHEEP ....... 169
Carlow Farmhouse
SEMI-SOFT/COW ................ 133
Cashel Blue BLUE/COW ........... 80
Cavanbert MOULD-RIPENED/COW.. 38
Cenarth Brie
MOULD-RIPENED/COW ........... 39
Cerwyn Mature HARD/COW ..... 170
Clerkland Crowdie FRESH/COW.. 19
Clonmore HARD/GOAT ........... 171
Colston Bassett Stilton
BLUE/COW ...................... 81
Coolattin HARD/COW ........... 172
Coolea HARD/COW .............. 173
Corleggy Kid
MOULD-RIPENED/GOAT ......... 40
Cornish Yarg SEMI-SOFT/COW . 134
Corra Linn HARD/SHEEP ....... 174
Cote Hill Blue BLUE/COW ........ 82
Cote Hill White FRESH/COW...... 20
Crookwheel SEMI-SOFT/SHEEP .. 135
Crozier Blue BLUE/COW .......... 83
Crump's Double Gloucester
HARD/COW .................... 175
Crump's Single Gloucester
SEMI-SOFT/COW ................ 136
Cuddy's Cave SEMI-SOFT/COW .. 137

Cumberland Farmhouse
HARD/COW ..................... 176

### D

Darling Blue BLUE/COW ........... 84
Derg Cheddar HARD/COW ....... 177
Doddington HARD/COW ......... 178
Dorset Blue Vinney BLUE/COW ... 85
Dorstone MOULD-RIPENED/GOAT ... 41
Drewi Sant WASHED-RIND/COW . 107
Drumlin HARD/COW ............. 179
Duckett's Caerphilly
SEMI-SOFT/COW ................. 138
Dunlop HARD/COW ............. 180
Dunmanus SEMI-SOFT/COW ..... 139
Durrus WASHED-RIND/COW ...... 108

### E

Edmund Tew
WASHED-RIND/COW ............. 109
Elmhirst MOULD-RIPENED/COW ... 42
Elrick Log MOULD-RIPENED/GOAT 43
Eve WASHED-RIND/GOAT ........ 110

### F

Fellstone (Whin Yeats
Wensleydale) SEMI-SOFT/COW 140
Fifteen Fields HARD/COW ....... 181
Flower Marie
MOULD-RIPENED/SHEEP .......... 44

### G

Goatisan HARD/GOAT ............ 182
Golden Cross
MOULD-RIPENED/GOAT .......... 45
Gorwydd Caerphilly
SEMI-SOFT/COW ................. 141
Gubbeen WASHED-RIND/COW .... 111

### H

Hafod HARD/COW ................ 183
Hardy's HARD/SHEEP ............ 184
Hebden MOULD-RIPENED/GOAT . 46
Hebridean Blue BLUE/COW ...... 86
Hegarty's Cheddar HARD/COW . 185
Highmoor WASHED-RIND/COW .. 112
Isle of Mull Cheddar HARD/COW 186

### K

Kedar Mozzarella FRESH/COW ... 21
Keen's Cheddar HARD/COW ..... 187
Killeen HARD/GOAT .............. 188
Kirkham's Lancashire
HARD/COW ..................... 189
Kit Calvert Wensleydale
HARD/COW ..................... 190

### L

Lanark Blue BLUE/SHEEP .......... 87
Leeds Blue BLUE/SHEEP .......... 88
Lincolnshire Poacher HARD/COW 191
Lindum WASHED-RIND/COW ..... 113
Little Hereford HARD/COW ...... 192
Little Rollright
WASHED-RIND/COW ............. 114
Little She MOULD-RIPENED/SHEEP 47
Loch Arthur HARD/COW ......... 193
Lord London
MOULD-RIPENED/COW .......... 48
Lord of the Hundreds
HARD/SHEEP ................... 194
Ludlow Blue BLUE/COW .......... 89

### M

Maida Vale WASHED-RIND/COW . 115
Martell's Double Gloucester
HARD/COW ..................... 195

Martell's Single Gloucester
SEMI-SOFT/COW .............. 142
Mayfield HARD/COW ............ 196
Merry Wyfe of Bath
WASHED-RIND/COW .......... 116
Milleens WASHED-RIND/COW .... 117
Mon Las Anglesey Blue
BLUE/COW ...................... 90
Monkland SEMI-SOFT/COW ...... 143
Montgomery's Cheddar
HARD/COW ..................... 197
Moorland Tomme
SEMI-SOFT/COW .............. 144
Mossfield HARD/COW ........... 198
Mrs. Bell's Blue BLUE/SHEEP ...... 91

N

Norfolk Dapple HARD/COW .... 199
Ogleshield WASHED-RIND/COW.. 118
Old Roan SEMI-SOFT/COW ....... 145
Old Winchester HARD/COW .... 200
Owd Ewe HARD/COW ............ 201
Oxford Blue BLUE/COW .......... 92
Oxford Isis WASHED-RIND/COW .. 119

P

Pant Ys Gawn FRESH/GOAT ...... 22
Perroche FRESH/GOAT ........... 23
Pitchfork Cheddar HARD/COW .. 202

Q

Quicke's Cheddar HARD/COW .. 203

R

Rachel WASHED-RIND/GOAT ...... 120
Ragstone MOULD-RIPENED/GOAT .. 49
Rainton Tomme SEMI-SOFT/COW .. 146

Remembered Hills BLUE/COW .... 93
Renegade Monk
WASHED-RIND/COW .......... 121
Richard III Wensleydale
SEMI-SOFT/COW .............. 147
Rockfield SEMI-SOFT/SHEEP ..... 148

S

St Andrews HARD/COW........... 204
Saint Cera WASHED-RIND/COW .. 122
Saint Gall HARD/COW ........... 205
Saint George
MOULD-RIPENED/GOAT ......... 50
Saint James
WASHED-RIND/SHEEP .......... 123
Saint Jude MOULD-RIPENED/COW.. 51
Saint Tola MOULD-RIPENED/GOAT.. 52
Saint Tola Ash
MOULD-RIPENED/GOAT ......... 53
Saval WASHED-RIND/COW ....... 124
Seator's Orkney SEMI-SOFT/COW 149
Shropshire HARD/COW .......... 206
Shropshire Blue BLUE/COW ...... 94
Sinodun Hill
MOULD-RIPENED/GOAT ......... 54
Sparkenhoe Blue BLUE/COW ...... 95
Sparkenhoe Red Leicester
HARD/COW ..................... 207
Spenwood HARD/SHEEP ......... 208
Stichelton BLUE/COW ............ 96
Stinking Bishop
WASHED-RIND/COW ............ 125
Stonebeck Wensleydale
SEMI-SOFT/COW .............. 150
Stoney Cross SEMI-SOFT/COW ... 151
Suffolk Gold SEMI-SOFT/COW .... 152
Summerfield HARD/COW ......... 209

## T

Teifi HARD/COW ................... 210
Templegall HARD/COW .......... 211
The Cheese With No Name
   MOULD-RIPENED/COW ............ 55
Thelma's Caerffili
   SEMI-SOFT/COW ............... 53
Ticklemore SEMI-SOFT/GOAT .... 154
Tinto HARD/GOAT ................ 212
Tor MOULD-RIPENED/GOAT ........ 56
Triple Rose MOULD-RIPENED/COW 57
Tunworth
   MOULD-RIPENED/COW ........... 58

## W

Wells Alpine HARD/COW ......... 213

Westcombe Cheddar HARD/COW 14
Westray Wife
   WASHED-RIND/COW ............. 126
Wicklow Bán
   MOULD-RIPENED/COW ............ 59
Wicklow Blue BLUE/COW ........ 97
Wigmore MOULD-RIPENED/SHEEP 60
Wiltshire Loaf SEMI-SOFT/COW 155
Winslade MOULD-RIPENED/COW.. 61
Witheridge MOULD-RIPENED/COW 62

## Y

Yorkshire Fettle FRESH/SHEEP .. 24
Yorkshire Pecorino
   SEMI-SOFT/SHEEP ............. 156
Young Buck BLUE/COW .......... 98

# Suitable for vegetarians?
## AN INDEX OF RENNETS

Rennet is an integral part of making nearly all cheeses: the rennet coagulates the milk and makes a firmer curd. Traditionally, most British cheesemakers used **animal rennet** derived from the lining of a calf's stomach. These days many use **vegetarian alternatives** derived either from the sap of the cardoon thistle, by fermenting certain fungi, or from modified microorganisms like yeasts or bacteria. It is not always clear, when buying cheese, whether it has been made with animal rennet (often called '**traditional rennet**') or vegetarian rennet. And I hold my hand up: after sending this book off to print, I noticed some errors (almost all noting animal rennet when vegetarian rennet is used; though **Gubbeen** and **Saint Jude** are noted as vegetarian when animal rennet is used).

So, below is an **index of rennets** used in all the cheeses in the *Compendium*. Please use this as your guide, rather than the rennets noted in the book. And if the type of rennet is important to you, do check packaging labels or ask your cheesemonger. Cheesemakers make changes from time to time – and just to confuse matters, a few cheesemakers make vegetarian and non-vegetarian versions of their cheeses; Colston Basset Stilton is one notable example.

## CHEESES MADE WITH VEGETARIAN RENNET

Ailsa Craig
Angiddy
Ballyhubbock Halloumi
Barkham Blue
Beenleigh Blue
Binham Blue
Bluemin White
Boyne Valley Blue
Brefu Bach
Buffalo Blue
Burts Blue
Caerfai Caerfili
Cashel Blue
Cavanbert
Cenarth Brie
Cerwyn Mature

The Cheese With
 No Name
Clerkland Crowdie
Clonmore
Colston Bassett Stilton
 [animal/vegetarian]
Corleggy Kid
Cornish Yarg
Cote Hill Blue
Crozier Blue
Crump's Double
 Gloucester
Crump's Single
 Gloucester
Dorset Blue Vinny
Drewi Sant

Drumlin
Dunlop
Elmhirst
Eve
Fifteen Fields
Flower Marie
Goatisan
Golden Cross
Hardy
Hebden
Hegarty's Cheddar
Kedar Cheese Co
 Mozzarella
Kit Calvert
 Wensleydale
Lanark Blue

Little She
Loch Arthur
Lord London
Lord of the Hundreds
Ludlow Blue
Maida Vale
Martell's Double
  Gloucester
Martell's Single
  Gloucester
Mayfield
Merry Wyfe
Mon Las Anglesea Blue
Moorland Tomme
Mossfield
Mrs Bell's Blue
Old Roan

Old Winchester
Owd Ewe
Oxford Blue
Oxford Isis
Pant Ys Gawn
Perroche
Rachel
Rainton Tomme
Remembered Hills
Renegade Monk
Richard III Wensleydale
Seator's Orkney
Shropshire Blue
Sinodun HIII
Spenwood
Saint George
Stinking Bishop

Stoney Cross
Suffolk Gold
Summerfield
Templegall
Thelma Caerfilli
Ticklemore
Tinto
Tor
Triple Rose
Well's Alpine
Westray Wife
Wicklow Bán
Wicklow Blue
Wigmore
Wiltshire Loaf
Winslade
Yorkshire Fettle

## CHEESES MADE WITH ANIMAL/TRADITIONAL RENNET

Admiral Collingwood
Allerdale
Anster
Applebys Cheshire
Baron Bigod
Baronet
Bath Blue
Beauvale
Berkswell
Bermondsey
  Hard Pressed
Bix
Blue Monk
Cais Na Tire
Carlow Farmhouse
Colston Bassett Stilton
  [animal/vegetarian]
Coolattin
Coolea
Corra Linn
Cote Hill White
Crookwheel
Cuddy's Cave
Cumberland Farmhouse
Darling Blue
Derg Cheddar

Doddington
Dorstone
Duckett's Caerphilly
Dunmanus
Durrus
Edmund Tew
Elrick Log
Fellstone (Whin Yeats)
Gorwydd Caerphilly
Gubbeen
Hafod
Hebridean Blue
Highmoor
Isle of Mull Cheddar
Keens Cheddar
Killeen
Kirkhams Lancashire
Leeds Blue
Lincolnshire Poacher
Lindum
Little Hereford
Little Rollright
Milleens
Monkland
Montgomery's Cheddar
Norfolk Dapple

Ogleshield
Pitchfork Cheddar
Quickes Cheddar
Ragstone
Rockfield
Saval
Shropshire
Sparkenhoe Blue
Sparkenhoe
  Red Leicester
St Andrews
Saint Cera
Saint Gall
Saint James
Saint Jude
Saint Tola
Saint Tola Ash
Stichelton
Stonebeck
Teifi
Tunworth
Westcombe
Witheridge
Yorkshire Pecorino
Young Buck

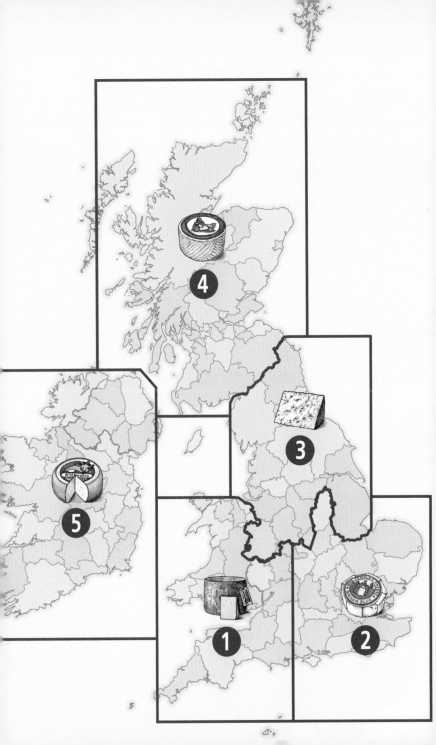

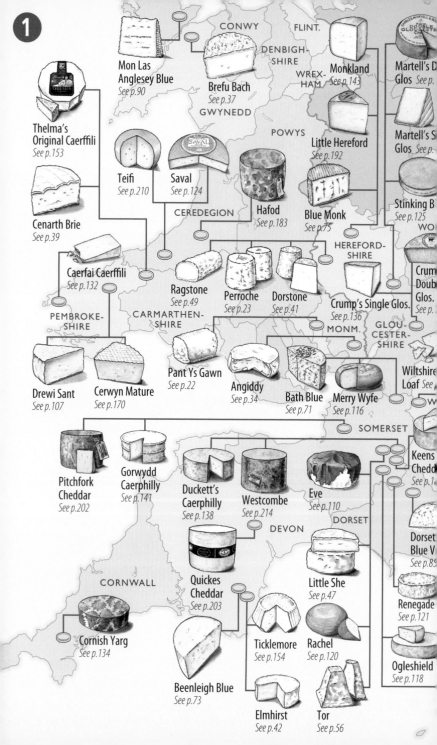

**1**

Mon Las
Anglesey Blue
*See p.90*

CONWY    FLINT.

DENBIGH-
SHIRE

Brefu Bach
*See p.37*

GWYNEDD

WREX-
HAM    Monkland
*See p.143*

Martell's D
Glos *See p.*

POWYS

Little Hereford
*See p.192*

Martell's S
Glos *See p.*

Thelma's
Original Caerffili
*See p.153*

Teifi
*See p.210*

Saval
*See p.124*

Hafod
*See p.183*

Blue Monk
*See p.75*

Stinking B
*See p.125*

WO

Cenarth Brie
*See p.39*

CEREDIGION

HEREFORD-
SHIRE

Crum
Doub
Glos.
*See p.*

Caerfai Caerffili
*See p.132*

Ragstone
*See p.49*

Perroche
*See p.23*

Dorstone
*See p.41*

Crump's Single Glos.
*See p.136*

GLOU-
CESTER-
SHIRE

PEMBROKE-
SHIRE

CARMARTHEN-
SHIRE

MONM.

Drewi Sant
*See p.107*

Cerwyn Mature
*See p.170*

Pant Ys Gawn
*See p.22*

Angiddy
*See p.34*

Bath Blue
*See p.71*

Merry Wyfe
*See p.116*

Wiltshire
Loaf *See*

W

SOMERSET

Pitchfork
Cheddar
*See p.202*

Gorwydd
Caerphilly
*See p.141*

Duckett's
Caerphilly
*See p.138*

Westcombe
*See p.214*

Eve *See p.110*

Keens
Chedd
*See p.1*

DEVON

DORSET

Quickes
Cheddar
*See p.203*

Little She
*See p.47*

Dorset
Blue V
*See p.89*

CORNWALL

Renegade
*See p.121*

Cornish Yarg
*See p.134*

Ticklemore
*See p.154*

Rachel
*See p.120*

Oglesfield
*See p.118*

Beenleigh Blue
*See p.73*

Elmhirst
*See p.42*

Tor
*See p.56*

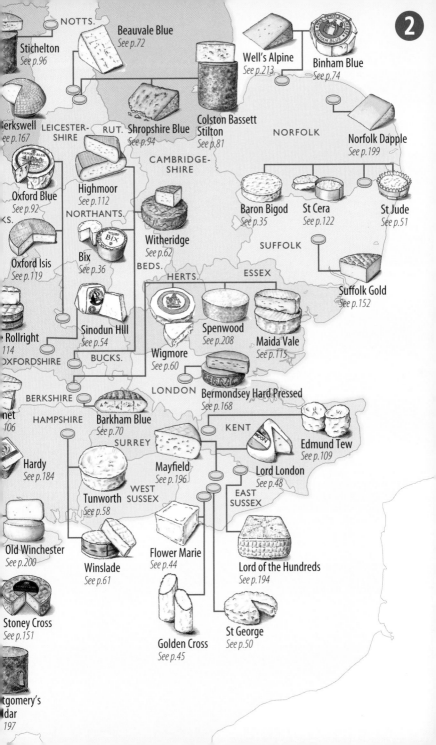

## 2

NOTTS.

Stichelton
*See p.96*

Beauvale Blue
*See p.72*

Well's Alpine
*See p.213*

Binham Blue
*See p.74*

erkswell
*ee p.167*

LEICESTER-
SHIRE

RUT.

Shropshire Blue
*See p.94*

Colston Bassett
Stilton
*See p.81*

NORFOLK

Norfolk Dapple
*See p.199*

Oxford Blue
*See p.92*

CAMBRIDGE-
SHIRE

Highmoor
*See p.112*

NORTHANTS.

Baron Bigod
*See p.35*

St Cera
*See p.122*

St Jude
*See p.51*

KS.

Oxford Isis
*See p.119*

Bix
*See p.36*

Witheridge
*See p.62*

SUFFOLK

BEDS.

HERTS.

ESSEX

Suffolk Gold
*See p.152*

Rollright
*114*

Sinodun Hill
*See p.54*

Wigmore
*See p.60*

Spenwood
*See p.208*

Maida Vale
*See p.115*

OXFORDSHIRE

BUCKS.

LONDON

Bermondsey Hard Pressed
*See p.168*

BERKSHIRE

net
*106*

HAMPSHIRE

Barkham Blue
*See p.70*

KENT

Edmund Tew
*See p.109*

Hardy
*See p.184*

SURREY

Mayfield
*See p.196*

Lord London
*See p.48*

Tunworth
*See p.58*

WEST
SUSSEX

EAST
SUSSEX

Old Winchester
*See p.200*

Winslade
*See p.61*

Flower Marie
*See p.44*

Lord of the Hundreds
*See p.194*

Stoney Cross
*See p.151*

Golden Cross
*See p.45*

St George
*See p.50*

tgomery's
dar
*197*

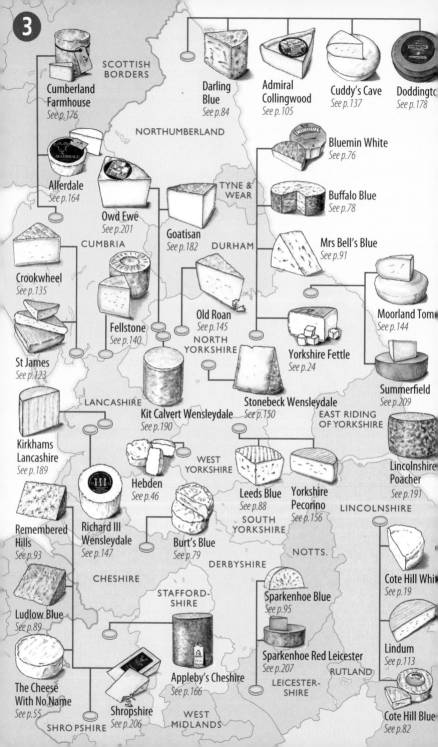

**3**

SCOTTISH BORDERS

Cumberland Farmhouse
*See p.176*

Darling Blue
*See p.84*

Admiral Collingwood
*See p.105*

Cuddy's Cave
*See p.137*

Doddington
*See p.178*

NORTHUMBERLAND

Bluemin White
*See p.76*

Allerdale
*See p.164*

Owd Ewe
*See p.201*

TYNE & WEAR

Buffalo Blue
*See p.78*

Goatisan
*See p.182*

DURHAM

Mrs Bell's Blue
*See p.91*

CUMBRIA

Crookwheel
*See p.135*

Fellstone
*See p.140*

Old Roan
*See p.145*

Moorland Tom
*See p.144*

NORTH YORKSHIRE

St James
*See p.123*

Yorkshire Fettle
*See p.24*

Summerfield
*See p.209*

Kit Calvert Wensleydale
*See p.190*

Stonebeck Wensleydale
*See p.150*

EAST RIDING OF YORKSHIRE

LANCASHIRE

Kirkhams Lancashire
*See p.189*

Hebden
*See p.46*

WEST YORKSHIRE

Lincolnshire Poacher
*See p.191*

Remembered Hills
*See p.93*

Richard III Wensleydale
*See p.147*

Burt's Blue
*See p.79*

Leeds Blue
*See p.88*

Yorkshire Pecorino
*See p.156*

SOUTH YORKSHIRE

LINCOLNSHIRE

NOTTS.

DERBYSHIRE

CHESHIRE

Ludlow Blue
*See p.89*

Cote Hill White
*See p.19*

STAFFORD-SHIRE

Sparkenhoe Blue
*See p.95*

The Cheese With No Name
*See p.55*

Lindum
*See p.113*

Appleby's Cheshire
*See p.166*

Sparkenhoe Red Leicester
*See p.207*

RUTLAND

LEICESTER-SHIRE

Shropshire
*See p.206*

WEST MIDLANDS

SHROPSHIRE

Cote Hill Blue
*See p.82*

**4**

Westray Wife
See p.126

ORKNEY

Seator's Orkney
See p.149

EAN
IAR

Hebridean Blue
See p.86

HIGHLAND

Lanark Blue
See p.87

MORAY

ABERDEENSHIRE

Tinto
See p.212

Isle of Mull Cheddar
See p.186

Elrick Log
See p.43

PERTH AND
KINROSS

ANGUS

St Andrews
See p.204

ARGYLL
AND BUTE

STIRLING

FIFE

Anster
See p.165

a Craig
.33

Clerkland Crowdie
See p.20

Dunlop
See p.180

Corra Linn
See p.174

LOTHIAN

SOUTH
LANARKSHIRE

SCOTTISH
BORDERS

EAST
AYRSHIRE

SOUTH
AYRSHIRE

DUMFRIES AND
GALLOWAY

NORTHERN
IRELAND

Rainton Tomme
See p.146

Loch Arthur
See p.193

Kedar Mozzarella
See p.21

**5**

ANTRIM

LONDONDERRY

DONEGAL

TYRONE

Young Buck
*See p.98*

Triple Rose
*See p.57*

FERMANAGH · ARMAGH · DOWN

Corleggy Kid
*See p.40*

Cavanbert
*See p.38*

Drumlin
*See p.179*

MONAGHAN

MAYO · SLIGO · LEITRIM · CAVAN · LOUTH

Rockfield
*See p.148*

ROSCOMMON

LONGFORD

WESTMEATH

MEATH

Boyne Valley Bl
*See p.77*

Cais Na Tire
*See p.169*

Mossfield
*See p.198*

DUBLIN

GALWAY

Killeen
*See p.188*

GALWAY

OFFALY · KILDARE

Ballyhubbock
Sheep's Halloum
*See p.18*

St Tola Ash
*See p.53*

CLARE

Derg Cheddar
*See p.177*

Coolattin
*See p.172*

LAOIS

WICKLOW

TIPPERARY

Carlow Farmhouse
*See p.133*

CARLOW

St Tola
*See p.52*

Clonmore
*See p.171*

Crozier Blue
*See p.83*

Cashel Blue
*See p.80*

KILKENNY

WEXFORD

Wicklow B
*See p.*

LIMERICK

KERRY

Milleens
*See p.117*

St Gall
*See p.205*

WATERFORD

Fifteen Fields
*See p.181*

Wicklow
*See p.*

CORK

Dunmanus
*See p.139*

Gubbeen
*See p.111*

Durrus
*See p.108*

Coolea
*See p.173*

Templegall
*See p.211*

Hegarty's
Cheddar
*See p.185*